CHRIST WITHOUT MYTH

SCHUBERT M. OGDEN

Christ without Myth

A STUDY BASED ON THE THEOLOGY
OF RUDOLF BULTMANN

Collins

ST JAMES'S PLACE, LONDON
1962

CONTENTS

Preface

The aim of this study is to contribute to the more adequate accomplishment of the basic constructive task confronting contemporary Protestant theology. That the larger part of it is devoted to an analysis and evaluation of the work of one man and of the other work his stimulation has called forth is in no sense incongruent with this aim. I have purposely sought to convey, by example as well as by precept, my deeply held conviction that all authentic theological work must take place within the church's ongoing conversation concerning the ultimate source of its common life. Though the theological task is never done and must constantly be undertaken *ab ovo*, none of us approaches the task alone, but each stands in the midst of a vast company whose presence is a constant inspiration—those who have gone before and those who will come after. Each of us begins his theological work with an inestimable debt to the past and an incalculable responsibility to the future, both of which drive him to do nothing more than try to learn from those who have preceded him so as to be able to pass to those who shall follow the precious heritage that all must ever seek more adequately to express. This study will have failed of its purpose if it does not succeed in conveying this profound sense of solidarity with all who attempt to labour at the perennial theological task.

This prompts me to add that, although I have frequently found it necessary to criticise those from whom I have tried to learn, my purpose has been to give more adequate expression to the very things they themselves were also trying to express. That I have managed consistently to realise this purpose and have always been successful where so many others have failed would be folly to pretend. But that I have tried to take seriously the various implications of the ninth commandment—which is also relevant for theological work!—and have attempted to turn every criticism to mutual advantage will, I hope, be apparent from the character of the following discussions.

Of the other things that might be mentioned in this preface, four have an obvious priority.

In the first place, I must acknowledge that the title of the study was first suggested to me by Hans Werner Bartsch's stimulating little book, *Christus ohne Mythos : Die Botschaft der Evangelien für Jedermann.*[1] Since Bartsch's apt title seemed to me to express succinctly the very thing I myself most wanted to say, I have had no hesitation in appropriating it, and I count it a privilege now to acknowledge its source.

Second, for reasons that have seemed to me compelling, I have been unable to make direct use of the available English translations of the German works referred to in this study. Although some of these translations are unchallengeably excellent (Kendrick Grobel's fine translation of Bultmann's *Theologie des Neuen Testaments* is a case in point), others are almost equally inferior and are therefore disqualified for the purposes of the present study. Nevertheless, since so many of these translations are becoming available and most of my readers might naturally find it expedient to use them, I have adopted the procedure of indicating in parentheses after the appropriate reference to the original text the corresponding pages in any English translation currently in use. It goes without saying that all quotations from writings originally appearing in German are my translations and should not be considered the responsibility of other translators. I need add only that here, as in my translation of Bultmann's shorter writings,[2] I have left the German word "*existentiell*" un-

---

[1] Stuttgart: Evangelisches Verlagswerk, 1953.
[2] *Existence and Faith: Shorter Writings of Rudolf Bultmann*, New York: Meridian Books, Inc., 1960.

translated. The reasons for this are given in the Preface to that earlier book, and Section IV of the present study provides sufficient discussion of the meaning of the word and of its counterpart " *existential* " to excuse the absence of any further comment here.

Third, I must direct attention to the Appendix and explain the reasons for its inclusion in the study. Within days after the present manuscript was forwarded to the publisher, I came into possession for the first time of John Macquarrie's *Scope of Demythologising : Bultmann and His Critics.*[3] Recognising at once that the structure and concern of Macquarrie's book are strikingly parallel to my own and that his is perhaps the most challenging discussion of the demythologising debate yet to appear in English, I was most concerned to take some account of it before my own study was finally published. Since, however, my manuscript was already completed, the most feasible way to accomplish this seemed to be by the addition of an appendix. I am confident that I speak for my editors as well as myself when I express the hope that by this means the value of the study will be further enhanced and its timeliness for our current discussions made even more obviously evident.

Fourth, I must express my gratitude to all who assisted in bringing this project to completion. Since in its original form the study was submitted as a doctoral dissertation to the theological faculty of the University of Chicago, my most obvious indebtedness is to the various teachers who contributed to its origination, especially to Professor Jaroslav J. Pelikan, who served so helpfully as my adviser. In addition, I owe particular thanks to Professor Bultmann, who was quick to respond to my inquiries at certain points along the way. The same is true of four of my colleagues at Perkins School of Theology who selflessly made available to me their several talents at different stages of the book's preparation. Professors

[3] New York: Harper & Brothers, 1961.

Preface

Edward C. Hobbs, now of the Church Divinity School of the Pacific, and Van A. Harvey have been my *Gesprächspartner* in innumerable discussions on the themes of the book and have provided support and encouragement in ways beyond their knowing or my telling. Hardly less helpful has been Professor Decherd H. Turner, Jr., who read the entire manuscript with painstaking care and made countless suggestions for improving its style. A similar service was performed for part of the manuscript by Professor Victor P. Furnish, who, in addition, made helpful comments about the argument of the first two chapters. I also think with much appreciation of the promptness and cheerful efficiency of my typists, Mrs. Anne W. Norris and Mrs. Dorothy Laughbaum. Finally, I acknowledge my deep debt to my wife, who read the final manuscript with a critical eye and otherwise assisted and supported me in the whole undertaking.

S. M. O.

Dallas, Texas

That we have found the Christ in *Jesus of Nazareth* is confirmed because all the manifestations of God's faithfulness are indications or prophecies of what has encountered us in *Jesus*. The hidden power of the law and the prophets is the Christ who encounters us in *Jesus*. The meaning of all religion is the redemption, the turn of the age, the resurrection, the invisibility of God that constrains us to silence in *Jesus*. The substance of all human happenings is the forgiveness under which they stand as it is proclaimed and embodied precisely in *Jesus*. No one need object that this power, this meaning, this substance is to be found not only in Jesus but elsewhere. For we ourselves affirm this very thing; indeed, precisely we *can* affirm it. What is known and found in Jesus is that God is found everywhere, that before and after Jesus mankind has been found by God; in him we have the criterion by which all finding and being found by God may be known as such and by which we can conceive this finding and being found as a truth of the eternal order. *Many* walk in the light of redemption, forgiveness, resurrection ; but that we *see* them walk, that we have eyes for them, we owe to *one*. In *his* light we see light.

And that it is *the Christ* we have found in Jesus is confirmed because Jesus is the final word, which clarifies all the others and brings them to sharpest expression, of the faithfulness of God to which the law and the prophets bear witness.

KARL BARTH, *Der Römerbrief*, pp. 72 f.

CHAPTER I

The Contemporary Theological Problem

I. THE SITUATION IN CONTEMPORARY PROTESTANT THEOLOGY

Of the many statements concerning the nature of theological work that have appeared in recent years, one of the most compelling is Karl Barth's in the opening pages of his study of nineteenth-century Protestant theology. With the discernment and eloquence his contemporaries have long since learned to expect of him, Barth points out that theology cannot consist merely " in ascertaining and communicating results already obtained in some classical period," but must consist rather " in a reflection that is constantly renewed " and therefore must " be undertaken again and again in complete seriousness and *ab ovo*."[1]

Barth also makes clear that this need for a constant return to origins does not mean that the theologian has to do his work in isolation or in a crippling dependence on his own resources. Rather, he says, even as we to-day pursue our task, " the theology of previous periods, both classical and less than classical, also speaks and demands a hearing." " Even with respect to theology, we cannot be in the church without responsibility confronting the theology of the past as well as

[1] *Die protestantische Theologie im 19. Jahrhundert*, Zollikon-Zürich: Evangelischer Verlag, 1952, p. 2.

the theology of our own present. Augustine, Thomas, Luther, Schleiermacher, and all the others are not dead but alive." "There are only relative heretics . . . [and] the theology of every present must be strong enough and free enough to listen calmly, attentively, and openly to *all* the voices of the past— and not only to those of the Fathers or of some classical period, or of our own special favourites."[2] Barth's further elaboration of the reason for participating in this conversation with the past is particularly significant. "We cannot anticipate," he argues, "which of our fellow-workers from out of the past are or are not welcome to us in our own work. It is always possible that we may in some sense have an especial need of a completely unexpected and at first wholly unwelcome voice."[3]

If one asks what makes Barth's words so persuasive, the answer seems obvious. They succeed in expressing with unusual aptness a kind of consensus that has gradually emerged in our postliberal theological situation. In insisting that theology must constantly be developed anew and *ab ovo*—as a direct response to the kerygma itself, rather than as a reiteration of some previous response to it—they voice one of the basic insights of contemporary theological reflection. Largely as a result of the historical-critical research of liberal theology, it is now widely recognised that the various formulations of Christian theology have been in each case conditioned by the historical situations out of which they arose, and therefore it is impossible to maintain the simple identification of kerygma with theology characteristic of the different types of orthodoxy. On the other hand, it is also widely agreed to-day that the constructive work of liberal theology has been shown to be inadequate, and the main reason for its inadequacy lay in its failure to carry on the kind of vital conversation with its past of which Barth so eloquently speaks.

To be sure, liberalism performed a useful function in undercutting the pretensions of orthodoxy and delivering the

[2] *Ibid.*, pp. 2 f.   [3] *Ibid.*, p. 3.

theology of the present from a servile dependence on the past. But it performed this service only in order to fall subject itself to the limitations of its own historical epoch. In trying to distinguish " the essence of Christianity " from its various historically conditioned expressions, liberal theology drew its critical standards from contemporary world-views and thus allowed modernisations of the Christian message that have been proved to be inadequate by a rigorous pursuit of its own historical method. Although it seems certain that Barth hardly intends his remarks to apply solely to liberalism, it is fair to assume that he has its weakness particularly in mind in cautioning against any attempt to " anticipate " which of the voices of the past may speak to us as we ourselves labour at the theological task.

In any case, the primary characteristic of the present situation in Protestant theology is the determination everywhere manifesting itself to work at the theological task with the understanding to which Barth has given expression. It is generally acknowledged that if theological work is to be pursued at all, it must attempt to explicate Christian faith in such a way as both to deal with the problems and tasks of the present and also to maintain constant conversation with analogous attempts made in the past. The concept of a *Normaldogmatik* is all but universally regarded as untenable ; and yet it is also widely recognised that the Christian faith has its own distinctive identity and that the sole business of the theologian is obediently to articulate this faith in and for his situation. Moreover, there is general agreement that success in this undertaking is directly proportional to the theologian's preserving an attitude of openness and teachability towards the theological work of his predecessors ; for, in principle at least, every serious attempt at theological formulation deserves a hearing and constitutes a constant challenge and resource for contemporary reflection.

But with this we have already touched on the second characteristic of the present theological situation. Although, as we have noted, subsequent work has radically questioned liberal theology's constructive formulations, the process by which this has been achieved has also involved certain perils of its own. In the call, which was first issued some forty years ago, to return from a preoccupation with criticism to a simple acceptance of the New Testament kerygma, there was from the beginning the danger that the positive accomplishments of liberal theology would be obscured or even undone. The history of the intervening years has again and again witnessed realisations of this danger. Not only have the results of nineteenth-century scholarship been rejected, but the historical method itself has been called in question. Even more importantly, the liberal insight that the world-picture of antiquity has been rendered untenable by our modern knowledge of man and his world has frequently been disregarded. Beguiled by its enthusiasm for " the strange new world within the Bible," twentieth-century theology has overlooked the ambiguity of that " strangeness " and so shut itself against the criticism with which modern culture continues to confront traditional theological formulations. It has assumed too readily that the possibility for the theology of the past to speak relevantly to the present is a possibility not only in principle, but also in fact. It has rarely asked itself whether the character of our modern situation may not make such an assumption gratuitous.

The encouraging thing is that this failure on the part of the main theological movement of our century has increasingly come to be recognised for what it is. In more recent theology, particularly since the Second World War, there has developed a growing appreciation for liberal theology's achievements and a consequent unwillingness to endorse any simple and indiscriminate condemnation of it. To be sure, there is widespread agreement that the theology of the present must go " beyond " liberalism. Yet it is also generally agreed that this can be accomplished in a relevant way only by positively carrying forward the aspects of liberalism's critical work that are of enduring importance. Indeed, it is just this disposition to be critical of liberal theology, and at the same time to accept the legitimate motives that were at work in it that is the second outstanding characteristic of contemporary Protestant theology.

Our situation to-day is defined both by the renewed determination to pursue theological work in obedience to the kerygma and in critical openness to the entire Christian past and also by the concern to do justice to liberal theology and, in particular, to face in all seriousness the fundamental problem with which the liberal theologians sought to deal. However unanimous contemporary theologians may be in sensing the need for a reappraisal of liberalism's constructive formulations, they exhibit little inclination either to reject its historical-critical method or to disregard its basic insight that our modern knowledge of the world involves a conclusive criticism of all prescientific modes of thought. They are quite willing to acknowledge that their only legitimate task is to articulate in an appropriate way the understanding of reality that is implicit in authentic Christian faith. But they are unwilling to take for granted that this task is still a real possibility. They refuse to overlook that the vast bulk of previous theological formulations has been definitively challenged by the picture of man and his world implicit in modern philosophy and the various natural and social sciences.

The conclusion that emerges from the preceding analysis is that anyone who would attempt to pursue the theologian's vocation in the present situation is faced with a specific constructive task. He must by all means do his work in obedience to the New Testament proclamation and with a critical loyalty to the entire theological tradition ; and yet he can do this responsibly only by also embracing the criticism of that tradition which arises with necessity out of modern man's picture of himself and his world. However much one may be led to criticise liberal theology's constructive efforts, he must remember that the situation to which he has to address himself is essentially the same as that to which the liberal theologians likewise sought to speak. And this means he must never forget that the new theology that he himself must be concerned to develop will in the nature of the case have to be a post-liberal and not a pre-liberal theology.

2. THE NATURE OF THE PRESENT STUDY

If our characterisation of the current situation in theology is correct, and if the problem facing us is to formulate a genuinely post-liberal theology, then we are in a position to make some important distinctions between the resources for theological work available to us at the present time. Although, as we have seen, every serious attempt at theological formulation is in principle significant for our work, this cannot mean that such significance is in each case equally great. On the contrary, the very nature of the theological task as an attempt to articulate the understanding implicit in faith in the present situation requires us to introduce distinctions. It is simply a fact that the resources at our disposal are of unequal importance for our particular problem. This is true even though we would do well to heed Barth's warning against attempting to anticipate with any finality which of the voices of the past can speak a relevant word to our situation.

Assuming that our analysis is correct, we may set forth the following criteria: A given essay at theological restatement is significant for the present situation to the extent to which (1) it recognises the nature of the contemporary constructive problem and is concerned to develop a comprehensive solution to it; and (2) the solution it actually develops is adequate, in the sense both of comprehending the major dimensions that any such solution should comprehend and of being internally self-consistent. A few illustrations may help to clarify what these criteria imply.

If a particular theology simply ignores the present problem, whether by continuing to affirm liberal formulations that are demonstrably untenable or by trying to resurrect patterns of thought that liberalism's critical work long since laid to rest, it has relatively less significance for our contemporary task. By contrast, a theology that evinces the concern to move beyond both liberalism and the subsequent reaction to it by critically appropriating the legitimate motives in each will clearly be an important resource for the rest of us who are moved by a similar concern.

The second criterion implies, however, that a proposal that exhibits this concern and yet fails adequately to implement it still falls far short of being a maximally significant resource. Insofar as a theologian proceeds unsystematically or simply deals with fragments of a solution, his work has less importance than it may fairly be expected to have. By the same token, an integral approach to the problem that embraces all the dimensions of an adequate solution and also displays their systematic interconnections approximates the maximum of significance.

But the final test of adequacy is whether the solution in question is also logically self-consistent. Although we may readily agree that consistency is not the sole criterion of importance and that an inconsistent theology may still be immensely significant, we must insist that consistency is a relevant test. Insofar as a theology fails in being consistent, it also fails in being a maximally significant resource for other efforts at constructive restatement.

The hypothesis originally guiding the present study was that the theological work of Rudolf Bultmann, when assessed in terms of these criteria, is of extraordinary significance. What began as a conjecture, made on the basis of a limited knowledge of Bultmann's thought, has since become a firm conviction supported by a sustained examination of his work. It has become increasingly evident that for one who is concerned with the present theological task there is no better way to begin than by attempting to come to terms with Bultmann's proposal. Of the many resources available to us, probably none is more significant if one considers its capacity for clarifying the problem with which contemporary theology is confronted and for suggesting the lines along which a comprehensive solution may be sought. In any case, this conviction is fundamental to the present study and must always be kept in mind if the study's basic structure is to be understood.

Conversely, however, the study as a whole should provide ample confirmation of the truth of this conviction. If we succeed in showing what we hope to show, it should be evident that Bultmann well understands the contemporary theological problem and is vitally interested in solving it, and that the solution he proposes has most of the marks of an adequate solution. To be sure, we are eventually going to argue that his proposal finally fails in being maximally significant because it cannot meet the test of logical self-consistency. But, as was suggested above, this can hardly be taken to mean that his theology is not of singular significance. One of the purposes of the following analysis is to make clear that, in spite of its lack of consistency, it actually has such significance.

This leads now to some further comments about the nature of our study. First of all, it should be noted that the basic aim of the study is not historical and critical but constructive. By this is meant that we are primarily interested in something more than simply understanding Bultmann's theology and subjecting it to critical analysis. Our primary purpose is to make some contribution towards solving the main theological problem of our time.

To be sure, we have expressed the conviction that probably the best way to approach this problem is through a critical appropriation of Bultmann's proposed solution. In keeping with this conviction, the larger part of our study is devoted to understanding and appraising his proposal. Nevertheless, it is imperative to recognise that this is all finally but a means to a constructive end. The only reason for considering Bultmann's theology at all is because it is an uncommonly significant resource for dealing with the contemporary theological problem.

But this means that there are not two tasks that confront us in the study, but three. In addition to trying to understand Bultmann's proposed solution (Chapter II), and then subjecting his proposal to critical analysis (Chapter III), we must also attempt to set forth at least the outlines of our own constructive alternative (Chapter IV).

In one sense, of course, the latter task would require developing something like a complete systematic theology or at least the kind of sketch for such a system that Bultmann has provided in his programmatic essay, "Neues Testament und Mythologie."[4] In the present study, however, no effort will be made to fulfil such an ideal requirement. Not only do limitations of competence and space make its fulfilment impossible, but there is another sense in which it is not even necessary. Because, as we shall argue, Bultmann himself has already provided the main ingredients of a constructive solution, it is sufficient simply to understand his proposal to see the direction in which a complete answer must be sought. Moreover, the decisive step towards finding such an answer is to become clear about the fundamental conditions by which it must be determined. If we can succeed in specifying these conditions and so outline a course for further work, we will have come a long way towards realising our final aim. In any case, all this study aspires to do by way of constructive contribution is to present such an outline.

[4] H. W. Bartsch (ed.), *Kerygma und Mythos*, Vol. 1, Hamburg: Herbert Reich-Evangelischer Verlag, 2nd ed., 1951, pp. 15-48 (English translation by R. H. Fuller in H. W. Bartsch [ed.], *Kerygma and Myth*, New York: Harper Torchbooks, 1961, pp. 1-44).

There is another comment, however, that we must make about our inquiry. Although our ultimate end is constructive, we have elected to pursue this end by means of a critical appropriation of Bultmann's proposal. This means that we must of necessity also become involved in the larger theological discussion that has come to centre in his work. For almost two decades now, much of the energy of the theological community has been expended in trying to understand and come to terms with his solution. Inevitably, therefore, our own study will be viewed against this background. Hence the question naturally arises as to its precise place in the larger discussion, and here two points need to be kept in mind.

In the first place, the extensive discussion of Bultmann's theology going on since the Second World War has been a generally fruitful discussion. Unlike some other theological controversies, the so-called "demythologising debate " has led to at least three positive consequences: (1) Bultmann's theology is now more widely understood than it was when the debate began ; (2) there is nothing short of a real consensus concerning the basic inconsistency of his proposal ; (3) attempts have been made to formulate alternatives to his solution that are also of real significance for the present theological task.

In the second place, however, this discussion may hardly be supposed to have exhausted its topic, since, in spite of its positive accomplishments, much still remains to be done. Although Bultmann's thought is more widely understood now than it was prior to the debate, misunderstandings of it still abound even in substantial analyses of his work. This is particularly true of the English-speaking contributions to the discussion. Because with rare exceptions these contributions have been based on a relatively narrow acquaintance with Bultmann's writings, the picture they present is often one-sided and even quite mistaken. On this ground alone, there is ample room for what the present study proposes to do. But a similar judgment must also be made about the various criticisms of Bultmann's proposal. Although there is widespread agreement that his programme is intrinsically problematic, a definitive criticism of its inconsistency is yet to be developed. Finally, there can be no doubt that the effort to formulate a tenable alternative to his position is far from being complete. The alternatives proposed have almost never been subjected to the same sort of criticism that Bultmann's own proposal has received. Yet, until this is done, it is hardly possible to make a responsible decision about a constructive solution.

In short, conditions arising out of the larger discussion of Bultmann's work also help to determine the nature of the present undertaking. In pursuing each of the three tasks with which the remainder of the study is concerned, we will attempt to enter into conversation with the other main discussions of Bultmann's theology. In Chapter II we will rely on earlier attempts at understanding and yet at the same time try to deal with some of the most widely current misunderstandings of Bultmann's position. In Chapter III our attempt at immanent criticism will acknowledge the validity of the emerging consensus concerning his proposal, but will also seek to present a more adequate criticism of this proposal than has yet been achieved. Finally, it will be necessary to preface the constructive statement to be essayed in Chapter IV with a summary criticism of the other proposed alternatives.

CHAPTER II

Bultmann's Proposed Solution

3. THE PROBLEM

In Section 1, the present theological situation was characterised and the task that confronts contemporary theology defined. Although this was done without explicit reference to Bultmann, the interpretation was profoundly dependent on his analysis. To this extent, therefore, we have presented Bultmann's understanding of our situation and its problem. Nevertheless, an integral understanding of his proposal requires a sharper focusing of the precise problem it is intended to solve.

We begin by considering the understanding of theology that Bultmann typically presupposes throughout his work. As he conceives it, the function of theology is to make explicit, in the sense of raising to the level of conceptual knowledge, the understanding of human existence implicit in the decision of Christian faith. This means that if theological work is properly pursued, it is neither speculative nor scientific in an " objective " sense, but rather *existentiell*, that is, a type of thinking inseparable from one's most immediate understanding of oneself as a person.[1] In trying to describe such *existentiell*

[1] Cf. Schubert M. Ogden(ed.), *Existence and Faith: Shorter Writings of Rudolf Bultmann*, New York: Meridian Books, Inc., 1960, p. 120; cf. also pp. 88 and 93 f.

thinking, Bultmann sometimes makes use of a formula of Adolf Schlatter and speaks of it as a mode of thought in which the " act of thinking " (*Denkakt*) remains inseparably connected with the " act of living " (*Lebensakt*).[2] This implies that faith itself is something other than " piety " or " feeling," indeed, that it is an understanding in its own right, so that theology to some extent is already implicit within it. In this sense, theology is " a movement of faith itself " in which the obedience of faith is further realised and so " perfected."[3] Thus, when John Macquarrie, in interpreting Bultmann's view in the light of the philosophy of Martin Heidegger, speaks of theology as " a kind of phenomenology of faith," he expresses exactly what is involved.[4] It is in just such a phenomenological analysis that the work of the theologian consists. He seeks to unfold as clearly and systematically as possible the *existentiell* self-understanding implicit in Christian faith.

Such a self-understanding, however, has a specific object and content. To the *fides qua creditur* there corresponds the *fides quæ creditur*.[5] Faith is not simply one among several possible self-understandings that can arise spontaneously out of human existence itself. Rather, it is a self-understanding that is realised only in response to the word of God encountered in the proclamation of Jesus Christ. It is always faith *in* the kerygma, in the revealed word expressed in the New Testament and made concretely present in the proclamation of the church. Hence it is necessarily dependent on the theological formulations of the past, especially those of the New Testament. Although theological propositions are never themselves

[2] Cf. *Theologie des Neuen Testaments*, Tübingen: J. C. B. Mohr, 3rd ed., 1958, pp. 588, 594, 599 (English translation by Kendrick Grobel in Rudolf Bultmann, *Theology of the New Testament*, New York: Charles Scribner's Sons, 1951, 1955, Vol. II, pp. 240, 246, 251).

[3] *Existence and Faith*, p. 97; cf. also *Glauben und Verstehen*, Vol. I, Tübingen: J. C. B. Mohr, 2nd ed., 1954, pp. 89 ff., 157, 181 ff.

[4] *An Existentialist Theology: A Comparison of Heidegger and Bultmann*, London: S.C.M. Press, Ltd., 1955, p. 6.

[5] Cf. *Glauben und Verstehen*, I, pp. 86-91.

the *object* of faith, but merely its *explication*, the word of God that *is* the object of faith is never encountered except in the form of some theological expression.[6] Therefore, if faith is to exist, it must take place as the obedient hearing of the word that speaks from the pages of the New Testament. It also follows that theology as the self-explication of faith will express the self-understanding awakened by *this* kerygmatic word. In this sense, theology is indeed *ministerium verbi divini*, for its sole norm is the revealed word of God that has its origin and legitimation in Holy Scripture; and the purpose of every genuine theological statement is to explicate the self-understanding, or, in different words, the *existentiell* understanding of God, the world, and man, that is the real content of the New Testament itself.[7]

If this understanding of the nature of theology is taken seriously, however, the contemporary theologian is faced with a fundamental problem. For him, just as for those to whom he speaks, the proclamation of the church in the conceptual form in which it encounters him in the New Testament and in the classical theological tradition, seems unintelligible, incredible, and irrelevant. According to Bultmann, any attempt at the present time to understand and express the Christian message must realise that the theological propositions of the New Testament are not understood by modern man because they reflect a mythological picture of the world that we to-day cannot share.

But what is meant by " a mythological world-picture " ? The best definition of " myth " that Bultmann has given is the one in his programmatic essay of 1941 :

> Myth is spoken of here in the sense in which it is understood by research in the history of religions. Mythology is that manner of representation in which the unworldly and divine [*das Unweltliche, Göttliche*] appears as the worldly and

---

[6] Cf. *Theologie des Neuen Testaments*, pp. 586 ff. (II, pp. 237 ff.).
[7] *Ibid.*, pp. 585 ff. (II, pp. 237 ff.).

human—or, in short, in which the transcendent appears as the immanent [*das Jenseitige als Diesseitiges*]. Thus, in the mythological manner of representation, God's transcendence is thought of as spatial distance. . . . " Myth " is not spoken of here, therefore, in that modern sense in accordance with which it means nothing more than ideology.[8]

Elsewhere, Bultmann has further clarified his usage in similar terms:

I understand by " myth " a very specific historical phenomenon and by " mythology " a specific manner of thinking. It is this phenomenon and this manner of thinking that are at issue in the discussion. I used the concept " myth " in the sense customary in the science of history and in the scientific study of religion. In this sense, myth is the report of an occurrence or an event in which supernatural or superhuman powers or persons are at work ; hence the fact that it is often defined simply as history of the gods. Mythical thinking refers specific phenomena and events to supernatural or " divine " powers that may be represented dynamistically or animistically or even as personal spirits or gods. Thus it excludes certain phenomena and events and also certain realms from the known and familiar and controllable course of worldly occurrences. . . . Myth objectifies the transcendent and thus makes it immanent [*der Mythos objektiviert das Jenseits zum Diesseits*]. In doing so, it also makes it disposable, as becomes evident from the fact that cult more and more becomes a procedure for influencing the deity, for avoiding its wrath and for obtaining its favour.[9]

[8] H. W. Bartsch (ed.), *Kerygma und Mythos*, Vol. I, Hamburg: Herbert Reich-Evangelischer Verlag, 2nd ed., 1951, p. 22, n. 2 (English translation by R. H. Fuller in H. W. Bartsch (ed.), *Kerygma and Myth*, New York: Harper Torchbooks, 1961, p. 10, n. 2).

[9] H. W. Bartsch (ed.), *Kerygma und Mythos*, Vol. II, Hamburg: Herbert Reich-Evangelischer Verlag, 1952, pp. 180, 184.

If we consider carefully what is said in these two passages, " myth," as Bultmann understands it, has three aspects.

First, it is " objective," or, as the second statement puts it, it " objectifies " the reality of which it speaks. This notion of the " objective " or of the process of thinking by which something is " objectified " is as important for Bultmann as for the entire neo-Kantian tradition, including contemporary existentialism, that provides the philosophical background of his thought. In the terms of this tradition, to refer to something as " objective " or as an " object " means that it falls within the subject-object correlation fundamental for all acts of theoretical cognition. Correspondingly, to " objectify " something is to bring it within this basic structure by making it the term of a specific cognitive relation. Thus, the lamp I see before me on my desk is an " object " and the act whereby I focus it, an " objectifying " act. Furthermore, any statements I make about the lamp, say, concerning the colour of its shade or the wattage of its bulb, are properly defined as " objective " statements.

According to Bultmann, the defining characteristic of myth, or of mythological thinking, is that it " objectifies " and thus speaks in " objective " statements about a reality that is not an " object." This non-objective reality, variously referred to as " the unworldly," " the divine," and " the transcendent," is given in man's self-experience as the ground and end of his own existence and of his immediately disposable world. Thus, Bultmann speaks of myth as knowing " about another reality than the reality of the world that comes under the view of science. It knows that the world and human life have their ground and limit in a power lying beyond everything to be found in the realm of human calculation and control, or, in other words, in a transcendent power."[10] In speaking about this transcendent power, however, myth reduces it to just one more factor in the known and disposable world.

[10] *Ibid.*, p. 183.

It " objectifies " the transcendent and thereby transforms what is really a qualitative difference from the world into a mere difference of degree. Bultmann generally illustrates this by the example given in the foregoing definition: When myth expresses the experience of God's transcendence, it pictures him as dwelling in a heaven spatially distant from the world. The same thing also takes place in apocalyptic eschatology, for here " the idea of the transcendence of God is imagined by means of the category of time."[11]

The second aspect of the idea of myth is that it fulfils an etiological function. It not only answers the question of the origin and goal of the world as such, but also explains unusual or astonishing phenomena within the world that cannot otherwise be accounted for. Thus, Bultmann points out, mythological thinking refers certain occurrences that we to-day regard as natural to supernatural or superhuman causes. It regards them as " miracles," that is, happenings that cannot be understood as following from known natural causes and therefore must be assigned to some transcendent causality.[12] Because myth serves this purpose of casual explanation, it is plausible to regard it as primitive science. It reckons with cause and effect in the manner of science, and does so in the " objectifying " way characteristic of scientific inquiry. Nevertheless, Bultmann cautions against assuming that myth and science are the same kind of thinking. " For mythical thinking, the world and the occurrences in it are ' open '—open, namely, to the incursion of transcendent powers. For scientific thinking, on the other hand, they are ' closed,' that is, closed against such an incursion of unworldly agents. In another sense, of course, they are also ' open ' for scientific thought, insofar as our knowledge of the world and its occurrences is always incomplete and unfinished."[13]

---

[11] *Jesus Christ and Mythology*, New York: Charles Scribner's Sons, 1958, p. 22.
[12] Cf. *Kerygma und Mythos*, II, pp. 182 ff. [13] *Ibid.*, p. 181.

The third aspect of Bultmann's concept of myth is implied in the first and the second. This is that myth always takes the form of a report or narrative of non-natural or supernatural occurrences. As Bultmann observes, the simplest definition of myth is that it is " history of the gods " (*Göttergeschichte*). For the mythological mind, there is always a " second " history alongside the history comprised of ordinary events. For instance, in addition to the historical struggles of men, there are the " mighty acts " of the divine recounted in the myths and celebrated in rite and custom. Also, certain events believed to have happened in the world are separated off and given a place in a " holy " history discontinuous with the history of everyday occurrences. According to Bultmann, the result of mythological thinking is to produce this second kind of history, a history that is different from " secular " history, and yet, by reason of its narrative form, is also similar to it.

On the basis of Bultmann's understanding of myth, we offer the following definition : " A mythological world-picture " is one in which (1) the non-objective reality that man experiences as the ground and limit of himself and his world is " objectified " and thus represented as but another part of the objective world ; (2) the origin and goal of the world as a whole, as well as certain happenings within it, are referred to non-natural, yet " objective " causes ; (3) the resulting complex of ideas comprising the picture takes the form of a double history.

When Bultmann says that the New Testament's world-picture is " mythological " (or " mythical "), he means that it displays these three characteristics.

First, the New Testament assumes, in common with Jewish apocalypticism and the Gnostic myth of redemption, that the world is divided into three levels or stories. The middle level of ordinary historical happenings is transcended on both sides by a "numinous" reality. Above it is heaven, the dwelling-place of God and the angels ; below it is hell, the sphere of

Satan and his demonic cohorts. But even though these latter realms are realms of the numinous, the New Testament pictures them as though they had a spatial relationship to the ordinary level of reality : it "objectifies" the transcendent by representing it as a sphere (or spheres) within the inclusive world of objective reality.[14]

Second, the New Testament constantly reckons with non-natural causes in explaining the origin and destiny of the world and certain phenomena within it. Not only does it see the origin of the world in an other-worldly power that precedes the world in time, and the world's goal in a cosmic catastrophe that even now is about to take place ; it also regards the everyday course of events as standing "open" to the intervention of divine and demonic agency. Miracles are almost commonplace, and both man himself and events more generally under the control of supernatural powers.[15]

Finally, the New Testament is characterised throughout by what we have referred to as a double history. Besides narratives about ordinary historical events, it contains reports of other-worldly or supernatural occurrences. It everywhere presupposes the Old Testament-Jewish mythology of creation and speaks in reportorial fashion of the woes of the last days, the resurrection of the dead, and the final judgment. Indeed, the phenomenon of double history is especially noticeable in the New Testament because of the peculiar character of its message. For although the salvation-event it proclaims is represented as a mythical occurrence, it is not mythical in the sense in which, for example, the cultic myths of the Hellenistic deities are. On the contrary, the same figure pictured in mythological terms as Messiah or as a pre-existent divine being is also the historical person Jesus of Nazareth. Thus, as Bultmann says, "the historical and the mythical are here peculiarly interlaced ; the historical Jesus whose father and mother are well known (John 6 : 42) is at the same time the

[14] Cf. *Kerygma und Mythos*, I, pp. 15 f. (pp. 1 f.).   [15] *Ibid.*

pre-existent Son of God; and alongside of the historical event of the cross there stands the resurrection, which is not an historical event at all."[16]

From these considerations, Bultmann concludes that the New Testament's world-picture is mythological. This means, he argues, that for the modern man who no longer thinks mythologically the theological propositions of the New Testament are unintelligible.

Before we can pursue this argument, however, it is necessary to give brief consideration to a criticism of Bultmann's view that continues to find expression in spite of his reply to it in the second volume of *Kerygma und Mythos*.

Several critics have made the charge that Bultmann's concept of myth is ambiguous. Ian Henderson, for example, writes that "it seems fair to say that Bultmann groups together a number of not particularly homogeneous elements under the heading of the mythological."[17] More recently, John Macquarrie, who in this as in other respects betrays his deep indebtedness to Henderson, has made a similar objection, arguing that the term "myth," as Bultmann uses it, "seems to be a very confused one."[18] According to Macquarrie, Bultmann's formal definition of myth is unsatisfactory on two counts. First, it "is scarcely a wide enough definition, for . . . there are secular myths, such as the Nazi myth of the master-race and the Marxist myth of the classless paradise into which the divine does not enter at all."[19] Second, it is incapable of accounting for Bultmann's own assertion that the world-picture of the New Testament is mythological. For Macquarrie asks, "What does [Bultmann] mean by myth in this sentence? He goes on . . . to speak of the flat earth under the vault of the firmament—in other words, the Babylonian cosmology. But this is not myth within the sense of his own

---

[16] *Ibid.*, p. 41 (p. 34).
[17] *Myth in the New Testament*, London: S.C.M. Press, Ltd., 1952, p. 46.
[18] *Op. cit.*, p. 166. [19] *Ibid.*, p. 167.

formal definition. It is primitive science or primitive world-view, not a description of the divine in terms of this world, but a description of this world itself as these early thinkers imagined it to be."[20] In view, then, of "this confusion in Bultmann's usage," Macquarrie argues we must take myth to include (1) what may be called "myth proper," that is, the representation of the divine and unworldly in human and worldly terms and (2) everything in the New Testament that presupposes the primitive scientific concepts of the first century.

What are we to say about this criticism? In the first place, Macquarrie's claim that Bultmann's concept of myth is too narrow is irrelevant in the light of Bultmann's explicit rejection of any so-called "wider" definition. Bultmann makes perfectly clear that he does not wish to use the concept of myth "in that modern sense in accordance with which it means nothing more than ideology."[21] To state, as Macquarrie does, that Bultmann's use is "confused" and then to proceed to support this statement by appealing to a definition that Bultmann rejects is to introduce confusion where confusion does not exist.

Bultmann has explicitly indicated that if others hold his concept of myth to be questionable and wish to understand something else by it, they are perfectly free to do so. But he also states that he himself uses the term with a specific meaning and that it is this meaning that must be understood if the discussion with him is not to lead away from the central point.[22] It may well be, as Macquarrie claims, that Bultmann's definition is too narrow, but that hardly warrants the charge of a confusion of usage. Macquarrie's criticism cannot be sustained.

But Macquarrie also finds a confusion in Bultmann's usage because the latter allegedly employs myth both to refer to a kind of thinking and speaking in which the non-objective is

[20] *Ibid.*   [21] Cf. also *Kerygma und Mythos,* II, p. 180, n. 2.
[22] *Ibid.,* p. 180.

objectified and also to designate certain primitive scientific ideas. Here, too, Macquarrie's interpretation is open to question. If our analysis of Bultmann's view is correct, Macquarrie can discern such confusion only because he fails to see that mythical thinking is both similar to that of science, and different from it. He overlooks Bultmann's concession of only limited validity to the claim that myth is really primitive science. Thus, when he argues that the New Testament's mythical world-picture is "Babylonian cosmology" or that it is "primitive world-view, not a description of the divine in terms of this world," he makes a distinction Bultmann himself not only never makes but actually rejects. Bultmann writes : "There have occasionally been protestations against my designation of the three-story world-picture as mythical. Now it is correct that a three-story world-picture does not in itself have to be mythical. Nevertheless, it actually is so insofar as it is encountered in the realm of mythical thinking. For both the upper and the lower stories are thought of as 'numinous' spheres, that is, as realms of a transcendent reality of either a divine or a demonic character. Thus it is not permissible to distinguish between myth and world-picture in the way in which Emil Brunner . . . and W. G. Kümmel . . . would like to do."[23] The attempt to distinguish between myth and world-picture, which, in the case of Brunner and Kümmel, Bultmann explicitly disallows, is precisely what lies behind Macquarrie's second count against Bultmann's concept of myth. Only because he imposes on Bultmann's view a distinction that Bultmann himself denies can he justify the claim that Bultmann's understanding of myth is ambiguous.

It is impossible here to consider the other similar criticisms of Bultmann's view that have frequently been made.[24] None

[23] *Ibid.*, p. 183, n. 2.
[24] Cf., e.g., the essay of F. K. Schumann in *Kerygma und Mythos*, I., pp. 190-202 (pp. 175-190); also the essays of Albrecht Oepke and Regin Prenter in *Kerygma und Mythos*, II, pp. 69-84 and 170-175. Most recently this criticism has been made by L. Malevez, *The Christian Message and Myth*, trans. by Olive

of the criticisms that we have examined, however, is any more successful than Macquarrie's in showing that Bultmann's concept of myth is unclear. In each case, this claim rests either on a failure to observe the specific sense in which Bultmann originally defines the term or on a misunderstanding of what he has subsequently written in clarification of it. Our conclusion, therefore, is that Bultmann's usage is thoroughly consistent and remains completely untouched by the charge of ambiguity. As long as one concedes him the right to use the term as he chooses to use it and at the same time gives due regard to his careful explanations of its meaning, there is no reason for claiming that his use of it is confused.

We turn now to Bultmann's statement that the New Testament's mythical world-picture can no longer be understood or accepted by modern man. According to the argument set forth in detail in "Neues Testament und Mythologie," and somewhat more simply in *Jesus Christ and Mythology*, the mythical world-picture is to-day unacceptable because of the definitive criticism of it implied in modern thinking.[25] Bultmann does not mean by this that the development of modern thought has rendered the New Testament world-picture completely valueless or that any one of the various world-views current in the modern world is to be accepted as absolute and exempt from criticism. It is quite possible that there are important truths contained in the mythical picture of the world that have been overlooked or obscured in a so-called "enlightened" age; and a criticism of the New Testament that simply assumes the validity of a world-view like naturalism or idealism has no theological significance. "The only criticism of the New Testament that can be relevant for

---

Wyon, London: S.C.M. Press, Ltd., 1958, pp. 68 ff., and Giovanni Miegge, *Gospel and Myth in the Theology of Rudolf Bultmann*, trans. by Stephen Neill, Richmond: John Knox Press, 1960, pp. 91 ff.

[25] Cf. *Kerygma und Mythos*, I, pp. 16-21 (pp. 3-8); cf. also *Jesus Christ and Mythology*, pp. 14-18, 35-40.

theology is the one that arises with *necessity* out of the situation of modern man."[26]   What must be taken seriously is the "common basis" necessarily presupposed by all the ways in which man today can understand himself in his world. According to Bultmann, what constitutes this basis is, "on the one hand, the world-picture formed by modern natural science and, on the other hand, the understanding man has of himself in accordance with which he understands himself to be a closed inner unity that does not stand open to the incursion of supernatural powers."[27]

Although myth and science are alike in that each is an objectifying mode of thought and is concerned with explaining the world and its phenomena, there is an important distinction between them.   Whereas the former refers the world and certain of its happenings to transcendent and supernatural causes, the latter repudiates such a procedure and looks upon the world as a lawfully ordered unity "closed" to the interference of non-natural agents.   This latter type of thinking, although only fully developed in modern science, is already "preformed" in the "work-thinking" (*Arbeitsdenken*) that is as primitive as existence itself.[28]

The idea of lawfulness or of "nature" lies implicitly or explicitly at the bottom of all our thinking and acting.   It is not an "interpretation of the world," a "judgment of the world," a "view of the world"—or, in short, some opinion with respect to it that is merely subjective or a matter of decision.   On the contrary, *it is something given with existence itself*.   We constantly act in such a way as to rely on the lawful connection of worldly occurrences; and precisely when we act responsibly, we do not reckon with such possibilities as that God can rescind the law of gravity and the like.   "The simple resolve to work includes the idea that the things on which we wish to work conform to a certain

[26] *Kerygma und Mythos*, I, p. 19 (p. 7).
[27] *Ibid.*   [28] Cf. *Kerygma und Mythos*, II, p. 180.

lawfulness in their origin and effect and that by thinking we can master this lawfulness" (Wilhelm Herrmann). Our intercourse with others, when we show them something, summon them to do something, etc., presupposes this idea of the lawful regularity of events. We only acknowledge as actual in the world what can be demonstrated to have a place in this lawful continuum, and we consider assertions that do not allow themselves to be controlled by this idea to be fantasies.[29]

The proof that the idea of lawfulness or causal order is implicit in existence itself is that this idea is even applied to "miracles." To be sure, the primitive mind refers miracles to another causality than the causality of everyday occurrences of which man disposes in the service of his existence. Since, however, the idea of a double causality is not really thinkable, God, as the higher cause, is simply represented as an agent who knows more and can do more than other agents. Once the latter penetrate his secrets, however (as is done, for example, by the magician), this merely quantitative superiority is overcome. Bultmann points out that the course of historical development is such that events originally considered supernatural are more and more understood in terms of the idea of "nature." The implicit notion of lawfulness is radically developed, and along with this the idea of miracle as an occurrence *contra naturam* is also more radically understood. At the same time, the impossibility of regarding such occurrences as actual becomes increasingly apparent. "The idea of miracle has become impossible for us to-day because we understand nature as a lawful occurrence and must therefore understand miracle as an event that breaks this lawful continuum. Such an idea . . . is no longer acceptable to us."[30]

Bultmann also points out that even when science seeks to

---

[29] *Glauben und Verstehen*, i, p. 215 (English translation by F. D. Gealy in " The Problem of Miracle," *Religion in Life*, Winter, 1957-1958, p. 64).

[30] *Ibid.*, p. 214 (p. 63).

give an ultimate explanation of the world, it does not do so in the manner of myth, but in the manner of the Greek philosophy of nature. That is, it inquires concerning the ἀρχή of the world in the double sense of beginning (*initium*) and origin (*principium*).[31] "The very fact that the origin of the world is now no longer sought, as in mythical thinking, in an other-worldly power or deity, which is represented as preceding the world in time, but rather is thought of as an immanent origin constantly present in the world serves to clarify the fundamental difference between mythical thinking and that of science."[32]

This picture in accordance with which the world is understood as a closed and lawfully regulated unity is necessarily presupposed by modern men who live in the midst of a scientific and technological civilisation. Primarily for this reason, no one to-day can seriously maintain the mythological world-picture of the New Testament. However much the *results* of scientific research change, the fundamental *method* of science and the picture of the world correlative with it remain constant. And it is *this* method and *this* world-picture that make the New Testament's mythology untenable.[33]

Bultmann's argument at this point should be carefully noted, since it has so frequently been misunderstood by other interpreters. Macquarrie, for example, has claimed that Bultmann "is still obsessed with the pseudo-scientific view of a closed universe that was popular half a century ago, and anything which does not fit into that tacitly assumed world-picture is, in his view, not acceptable to the modern mind and assigned to the realm of myth."[34] Long before Macquarrie made this charge, however, Bultmann had replied to such criticisms with a telling argument. "Has the natural science of to-day renounced experimentation ? As long as it does not,

---

[31] Cf. *Existence and Faith*, p. 211.   [32] *Kerygma und Mythos*, II, pp. 180 f.
[33] Cf. *ibid.*, p. 181; cf. also *Jesus Christ and Mythology*, pp. 37 f.
[34] *Op. cit.*, p. 168.

it stands in the tradition of thinking that goes back to the Greeks with their question concerning the ἀρχή and their demand for the λόγον διδόναι. Whoever stands in this tradition also knows that all of the results of science are relative and that the particular world-picture of yesterday, to-day, or to-morrow can never be finally valid. But the decisive thing is not the results of scientific thinking, but its method."[35]

This statement leaves no doubt that a criticism such as Macquarrie's rests on a basic misunderstanding of Bultmann's point. His argument cannot be avoided by simply pointing out what he is fully aware of, that the world-picture of contemporary science is in certain respects different from that of the nineteenth century. The distinction between the naïve kind of thinking represented by myth and the critical procedures of *all* modern science is far more fundamental than any such difference. It is to *this* distinction, rather than to that kind of difference, that Bultmann calls attention.[36] Because man to-day is inevitably led to think in the critical manner of modern science, all that the biblical writings have to say regarding miracles or other worlds "above" or "below" the world of nature strikes him as incredible. The only way in which he can possibly affirm any of the contents of the New Testament's "second" history is by paying the fearful price of the *sacrificium intellectus* ; that is, he must violate the conditions for the integrity of his personal life by affirming as true what his own deepest understanding of the world belies.[37]

Bultmann does not deny that there are exceptions to this rule in the form of superstition and the survival of a certain amount of prescientific thinking. Macquarrie's statement that Bultmann ignores "the fact that in this scientific age thousands go to Lourdes every year, and that in Protestant churches also

---

[35] *Kerygma und Mythos*, II, p. 181.

[36] Cf. the statement by Christian Hartlich and Walter Sachs that Bultmann quotes with approval, *ibid.*, n. 1.

[37] *Kerygma und Mythos*, I, pp. 17 f. (pp. 3 ff.); cf. also *Jesus Christ and Mythology*, pp. 14-18.

there is a very real interest in what is called spiritual healing"[38] is simply untrue. As early as his programmatic essay, Bultmann gave indication that he was fully aware of the existence of such phenomena.[39] Still, as he argued there and has even more forcefully argued in later writings, what is important about such phenomena is that they are *exceptions*.[40] If one considers the prevailing tendencies in the over-all situation, rather than isolated cases, the unavoidable conclusion is that the decisive determinant in contemporary man's understanding of the world is the picture presented to him by modern science. What confronts him through "the school, the press, the radio, the movies, and technology in general" is precisely this picture.[41]

However, the New Testament is open to criticism for another reason than the scientific world-picture. According to Bultmann, modern man understands *himself* in such a way as to be unable to comprehend or accept many of its assertions.[42] Whether man to-day understands himself completely as nature or, in the manner of idealism, distinguishes his true self from nature, the one thing he cannot do is to view himself after the fashion of the New Testament myths as "open" to the seizure of alien and supernatural powers. He views himself, rather, as a unified being and attributes his experience, thought and volition to his own agency, not to divine or demonic causes. If, as a naturalist, he acknowledges himself in the highest degree dependent, he still does not look upon this dependence as a subjection to strange powers distinguishable from the orderly processes of nature. On the other hand, if he understands himself as "spirit," he is aware of his own freedom and responsibility, and even though he recognises his conditioning by natural forces, he distinguishes his true being from them.

[38] *Op. cit.*, p. 168.   [39] Cf. *Kerygma und Mythos*, I, p. 18, n. 1 (p. 5, n. 1).
[40] Cf., e.g., *Jesus Christ and Mythology*, p. 16; also pp. 36 f.
[41] Cf. *Kerygma und Mhthos*, I, p. 18, n. 1 (p. 5, n. 1).
[42] Cf. *ibid.*, pp. 18 f. (pp. 5 f.); cf. also *Kerygma und Mythos*, II, pp. 181 f.

In either case, what the New Testament has to say concerning the Spirit and the sacraments is completely unintelligible to him. The same is true of the idea of death as the punishment for sin. For both the naturalist and the idealist such an idea is incredible, since it contradicts the obvious fact that death is a simple and necessary natural process. Moreover, since they can only understand guilt, if they can understand it at all, as an act for which man himself is personally responsible, the mythological notions of original sin and substitutionary atonement are to them submoral and impossible.[43]

Finally, modern man finds it impossible to understand how a quasi-natural process like the dying and rising of a divine being can be the means for redeeming and fulfilling his life. Even where, as in the case of the idealist, it is meaningful to speak of such fulfilment, the notion that it is created by a remote cosmic occurrence is utterly unintelligible. "For [modern man] could see God's act only in an occurrence that took hold of the reality of his own true life and transformed him himself. But a miraculous natural event such as the resuscitation of a dead man—quite apart from its general incredibility—he cannot understand as an act of God of any concern to him."[44]

This last statement brings us to the heart of the criticism based on contemporary man's understanding of himself. If the general effect of the scientific world-picture is to render the New Testament's "second" history incredible, the essential thing about modern man's *self*-understanding is that it makes this "second" history irrelevant. Man to-day, Bultmann writes, "can understand himself in his relation to God only as a person who is addressed by God precisely in his being as a person. This means that the only divine speaking and acting he can understand as important and of concern to him are such as encounter him in his personal existence—and, in

[43] Cf. *ibid.*, pp. 19 f. (pp. 6 ff.).   [44] *Ibid.*, p. 20 (p. 8).

fact, adhere precisely to it."[45] Elsewhere, Bultmann argues that the supernatural situation depicted by the New Testament when it speaks of God's act in the mythological categories of Gnosticism is "not only rationally unimaginable" by man today, but also "says absolutely nothing to him. For he cannot understand that his salvation, . . . his authentic existence, should consist in such a condition."[46]

To summarise our discussion : First, there is a criticism of the New Testament that arises with necessity out of the historical situation of modern man. Second, the two characteristics of this situation (or, alternatively, the two conditions that determine the criticism) are the picture of the world formed by modern science and man's understanding of himself as a closed inner unity. And, third, the material in the New Testament open to such criticism includes: (1) everything that cannot be affirmed to have happened because it cannot be established in accordance with the general requirements of scientific research ; (2) everything that violates the unity of man's selfhood by representing him as "open" to divine or demonic powers whose agency is independent of his own responsible decisions.

That this criticism of the New Testament results in a complete destruction of the traditional Christian conception of "the history of salvation" Bultmann is well aware. Nevertheless, because it is a criticism arising from our situation *with necessity*, he insists theology has no alternative but to accept it. The theologian is forced to ask "whether the proclamation of the New Testament has a truth independent of the mythical world-picture."[47] He must ask this question with utter seriousness, for he cannot possibly hope to preserve the kerygma simply by eliminating the more obviously unacceptable elements in the New Testament mythology. Although not all of these elements are equally central (the legends of the virgin

---

[45] *Kerygma und Mythos*, ii, p. 182.   [47] *Ibid.*, p. 16 (p. 3).
[46] *Kerygma und Mythos*, i, p. 21 (p. 8).

birth and the ascension, for example, are not to be found in Paul and John), the elimination of some of the more peripheral ones changes nothing with respect to the fundamental problem —that the salvation-occurrence is *everywhere* represented in mythical terms.[48]

Furthermore, it is impossible to set methodologically defensible limits to such a picking and choosing procedure. In a brief reply to the criticisms of Karl Barth, Bultmann asks : "What elements, then, are contained in the mythical world-picture, which we, to be sure, do not need to maintain as a whole, but from which we can eclectically appropriate ? To inquire about a valid meaning of the mythical world-picture is precisely the intention of my existential interpretation, and in implementing this intention I attempt to proceed methodically. In the case of Barth, however, all I can find are arbitrary assertions. What is his principle of selection ?"[49]

It is because of the arbitrary procedure represented by Barth and others that Bultmann formulates the question in radical terms : "One must either accept or reject the mythical world-picture as a whole."[50] Moreover, he insists that if one does reject it, he must be perfectly clear about what he is doing and have no illusions about the critical character of his rejection. To demythologise unconsciously, as is often done by those who defend the indispensability of myth as the language of faith, is to fail to fulfil one's responsibility. "In many cases, we unintentionally and unreflectively demythologise the Bible's mythological statements by taking them as figures that have long since lost their original mythological meaning. . . . Whoever is charged with interpreting Scripture responsibly, however, should be conscious of what

[48] *Ibid.*, p. 21 (p. 9). Cf. *Kerygma und Mythos*, II, p. 185.

[49] *Glauben und Verstehen*, Vol. II, Tübingen: J. C. B. Mohr, 1952, p. 235 (English translation by J. C. G. Greig in Rudolf Bultmann, *Essays, Philosophical and Theological*, London: S.C.M. Press, Ltd., 1955, p. 261).

[50] *Kerygma und Mythos*, I, p. 21 (p. 9).

he is doing and say to himself that honesty requires that he be radical."[51]

Even less legitimate is the attempt to avoid a criticism of the New Testament by consciously or unconsciously reinterpreting its assertions in obviously forced ways. When Karl Barth in *Die Auferstehung der Toten*, for example, seeks to replace the future that Paul expects as an imminent cosmic occurrence with a *futurum æternum*, he clearly interprets Paul in a critical way. According to Bultmann, Barth can deceive himself and others into thinking otherwise only because he has already eliminated the mythological elements in First Corinthians by a highly artificial exegesis.[52]

Once one recognises, however, that all such partial or surreptitious attempts to deal with the New Testament's mythology are impossible, the task of theology is unmistakable. "If the New Testament proclamation is to maintain its validity, there is nothing else to do but demythologise it."[53] To be sure, Bultmann makes clear that such interpretation cannot be undertaken simply on the basis of the postulate that the New Testament's message must at all costs be made relevant to the present. On the contrary, "it simply has to be asked whether [this message] really is nothing but myth or whether the very attempt to understand it in its true intention leads to myth's elimination."[54]

As we pointed out at the beginning of the section, the only norm for theological work that Bultmann is willing to accept is the revealed word of God expressed in the New Testament. Consequently, he holds it is possible for the theologian to demythologise the kerygma only if the kerygma itself allows such interpretation. Although this does not mean that the kerygma is the *only* reason for demythologisation, it does mean that unless the New Testament message admits of this

[51] *Kerygma und Mythos*, II, p. 187.
[52] Cf. *Kerygma und Mythos*, I, pp. 21 f. (pp. 9 f.); cf. also Bultmann's extensive review of Barth's commentary in *Glauben und Verstehen*, I, pp. 57 and 63.
[53] *Kerygma und Mythos*, I, p. 22 (p. 10). [54] *Ibid.*

procedure, theology as the obedient response to this message becomes impossible. Since the criticism of the New Testament arising from our situation cannot be avoided, theology can continue to be a possibility only if the obedience of faith itself makes room for this criticism.

Is there, then, a solution to the theologian's problem ? Bultmann holds that two considerations encourage an affirmative answer to this question.

In the first place, "the true meaning of myth is not to present an objective world-picture," but to express "how man understands himself in his world."[55]

> Myth speaks of the power or powers that man experiences as the ground and limit of his world and of his own action and passion. . . . What finds expression in [it] is the faith that the known and disposable world in which man lives does not have its ground and aim in itself, but in the uncanny powers that lie outside of what is known and disposable and constantly control and threaten it as its ground and limit. In unity with this, myth also expresses the knowledge that man is not lord over himself, and that he is not only dependent within the known world, but is especially dependent upon the powers that hold sway beyond it. Myth also gives expression to the knowledge that it is precisely in dependence on these transcendent powers that man can become free of the powers that are known.[56]

In other words, myth intends to express "a certain understanding of human existence."[57] Although, as we have seen, myth objectifies the reality of which it speaks and in consequence represents this reality inadequately, its "true intention" does not lie in its objective contents, but in the understanding of existence these contents seek to express. "Therefore, in myth itself is contained the motive for criticising it, that is, its objective representations ; for its true intention to speak of a transcendent power to which man and the world are sub-

[55] *Ibid.*   [56] *Ibid.*, pp. 22 f. (pp. 10 f.).   [57] *Jesus Christ and Mythology*, p. 19.

ject is hampered and obscured by the objectifying character of its own assertions."[58]

But this implies that the mythology of the New Testament also is not to be interpreted in terms of its objective statements, but in terms of the self-understanding to which they give expression. "What is at issue is the question concerning the truth of this understanding of existence; and faith affirms this truth even though it may not be bound by the New Testament's world of representations."[59]

This first point is reinforced, however, by a second consideration. In the New Testament itself the way is already prepared for a criticism of its mythological assertions. The evidence for this, Bultmann believes, is threefold.

First, many of the mythological assertions in the New Testament either stand beside one another in a loose and unintegrated way or are positively self-contradictory. Second, "criticism is especially demanded by a peculiar contradiction that runs throughout the whole New Testament: On the one hand, man is cosmically determined; on the other hand, he is called to decision. On the one hand, sin is a fate; on the other hand, it is guilt. Alongside of the Pauline indicative stands the imperative, etc. In short, man is understood, on the one hand, as a cosmic being and, on the other hand, as an independent self who can win or lose himself in decision."[60] Bultmann adds significantly: "Hence the fact that many of the words of the New Testament directly speak to the man of to-day, while others are unintelligible to him."[61] Not only is it impossible for modern man to understand himself as a cosmic being (in the sense, of course, of the mythical world-picture); he is not even consistently understood in this way by the New Testament itself. As a matter of fact, a careful analysis of the text discloses that it is the latter element—the understanding of man as a free and responsible self—that is

[58] *Kerygma und Mythos*, i, p. 23 (p. 11).   [59] *Ibid.*   [60] *Ibid.* (pp. 11 f.).
[61] *Ibid.* (p. 12).

really determinative. Consequently, it is possible, and even necessary, that the former mythological element should be critically eliminated. Finally, however, "demythologisation is to some extent already carried out within the New Testament itself."[62] One needs only to note how John completely eliminates the futuristic eschatology of the primitive community to realise that the canonical writers themselves were far from being uncritical of the mythical world-picture.

Bultmann concludes that both the nature of myth in general and the New Testament in particular suggest the possibility, and even the necessity, of a critical interpretation of the New Testament mythology. However real the present theological problem is, there are these two indications that a solution can be found.

Even so, Bultmann acknowledges one important fact that should give us pause. Since the situation that occasions the demand for demythologisation is by no means a new situation, the attempt to interpret the New Testament so as to eliminate its mythological elements also is not new. Indeed, most of the theological work of the nineteenth century was motivated by the concern to demythologise the New Testament message. It is now commonly recognised, however, that these previous attempts at demythologisation failed to accomplish their aim. The liberal theologians succeeded in restating the kerygma only at the cost of eliminating or at least obscuring its very centre.

Thus, among the earlier liberals—for example, Adolf Harnack—the characteristic method of dealing with the biblical myths was simply to eliminate them as time-conditioned and dispensable and to look for the essential element in the great moral and religious ideas they inadequately express. In this way, the kerygma was reduced to a "world-view" (*Weltanschauung*), a body of timeless truths that have only an accidental relationship to the historical person or epoch

[62] *Ibid.*

through which they are first brought to consciousness. But this meant that the kerygma itself was actually eliminated. For the New Testament does not speak of Jesus Christ primarily as the great ethical and religious teacher, but proclaims him as the decisive event through which God has achieved man's salvation. In doing this, it does speak of Jesus' person in mythological terms ; but this in no way alters the fact that simply to eliminate this proclamation, as the early liberals in effect did, is to tear at the vitals of its message.[63]

A similar judgment must be made, Bultmann believes, concerning the demythologisation of the later "history of religions school." Although the members of this school recognised the inadequacy of the earlier liberal view of religion as "world-view" and sought to correct it by interpreting religion mystically as "feeling" or "piety," they were equally unsuccessful in appropriately restating the New Testament message. Here, too, the essential element was found in something finally independent of the historical event Jesus of Nazareth. According to Ernst Troeltsch, who is representative of the position, Christ is at best an imperishable cultic symbol.[64] Consequently, faith is not understood as faith *in* Christ, and all talk of him as God's decisive eschatological act must cease.[65]

It is small wonder, then, that the theology of the last forty years has so resolutely turned aside from the work of its predecessors and sought to find its way back to a simple acceptance of the New Testament message. Nevertheless, Bultmann holds that just because this is so, theology to-day is again in danger of becoming an impossible undertaking. However wrong the critical theologians may have been in their con-

[63] *Ibid.*, pp. 24 f. (pp. 13 f.). Cf., however, Bultmann's Foreword to the fiftieth anniversary edition of Adolf Harnack's *Wesen des Christentums*, Stuttgart: Ehrenfried Klotz Verlag, 1950, pp. vii-xvi (English translation by Salvator Attanasio and Ephraim Fischoff in Adolf Harnack, *What is Christianity?* New York: Harper Torchbooks, 1957, pp. vii-xviii).

[64] Ernst Troeltsch, *Die Bedeutung der Geschichtlichkeit Jesu für den Glauben*, Tübingen: J. C. B. Mohr, 1911, p. 30; cf. also pp. 14 f.

[65] Cf. *Kerygma und Mythos*, I, pp. 25 f. (pp. 14 f.).

structive statements, they were completely right in accepting the challenge with which the modern world confronted them and in recognising that the continued existence of the church and its message depends on a radical criticism of theology's traditional formulations.

Therefore, we to-day have no other alternative than to attempt once more the task of demythologisation they attempted. The question confronting us is clear, and on the answer to it hangs the fate of the Christian mission in the modern world: "Can there be a demythologising interpretation that discloses the truth of the kerygma as kerygma for the man who no longer thinks mythologically?"[66]

Bultmann's answer to this question is emphatically affirmative. It is his judgment, arrived at only after the most searching analysis and reflection, that a demythologised kerygma is a possible project and that this is true in spite of the obvious failure of previous attempts to carry it out.[67] Precisely when one approaches the New Testament myths "existentially," that is, not as objective reports of extraordinary phenomena, but as vehicles of a word that speaks out of existence and to existence, a tenable solution to the theological problem begins to appear. Indeed, Bultmann is convinced not only that the problem of theology is solvable, but also that *the existential interpretation required to solve it is something the kerygma itself demands*. Since this point has been so uniformly obscured by Bultmann's previous interpreters, we may further underline its importance by citing his own unambiguous statement.

[66] *Ibid.*, p. 26 (p. 15).
[67] It should be noted that Bultmann sometimes speaks of other unsatisfactory attempts at demythologisation than those of liberal theology; e.g., allegorical interpretation (cf. *ibid.*, p. 24 [pp. 12 f.]), the sacramentalism of Catholic Christianity, and the secularisation of eschatology by Hegel and Marx. Cf. Günther Bornkamm, Rudolf Bultmann, and F. K. Schumann, *Die christliche Hoffnung und das Problem der Entmythologisierung*, Stuttgart: Evangelisches Verlagswerk, 1954, pp. 26-32 (English translation by Conrad Bonifazi in " The Christian Hope and the Problem of Demythologising," *Expository Times*, May, June, 1954, pp. 230, 276 ff.).

If the task of demythologisation was originally demanded by the conflict between the world-picture of the Bible and the world-picture formed by scientific thinking, it soon became evident that *demythologisation is a demand of faith itself.* For the latter *requires to be freed from every world-picture sketched by objectifying thinking*, whether it be that of myth or that of science. The conflict between science and myth indicates that faith has not yet found its really adequate form of expression. . . . The criticism of the Bible's mythological world-picture and of the church's traditional proclamation arising from the modern picture of the world performs the great service for faith of calling it back to a radical reflection on its own true nature. It is this call that demythologisation wants to follow.[68]

Thus, so far from being an impasse, the present situation provides an unparalleled opportunity for reapprehending the true meaning of the Christian message and finding an appropriate form in which to express it.

4. THE PROJECT OF EXISTENTIAL INTERPRETATION

In summarising his position in relation to the attempts at demythologisation undertaken in the nineteenth century, Bultmann writes : "If one can say in a schematic way that in the epoch of critical research the mythology of the New Testament was simply *eliminated*, one can also say schematically that the task that faces us to-day is that of critically *interpreting* this mythology. Although this is not to assert, of course, that there may not also be mythological elements that require to be eliminated, it is to affirm that the criterion on the basis of which any such eliminations are to be made must be derived

---

[68] *Kerygma und Mythos*, II, p. 207 (English translation by R. H. Fuller in H. W. Bartsch [ed.], *Kerygma and Myth*, New York: Harper Torchbooks, 1961, p. 210). Cf. also *Jesus Christ and Mythology*, p. 83.

from the understanding of existence of the New Testament itself rather than from the modern world-view."[69] In other words, what is required of contemporary theology is an "existential interpretation" of the New Testament mythology. According to Bultmann, if we are to avoid the mistakes of liberal theology and yet at the same time deal with the problem presented by the New Testament world-picture, we must devote ourselves to interpreting the biblical myths critically in terms of the *existentiell* understanding of existence they basically seek to express.

In order to understand what this claim implies, it is necessary to examine the methodological foundations of Bultmann's constructive proposal. Specifically, we must (1) grasp at least the basic structure of his view of man and (2) understand the general theory of hermeneutics with which this view is most closely connected.

For Bultmann, the being of man is inadequately understood as long as he is considered as a "what" or "object" whose properties may be more or less completely described by a perceptive observer. In common with the contemporary existentialist philosophers, Bultmann insists that man's nature is clearly focused only when he is regarded as a "who" or "person" ultimately eluding every such attempt at objective description. Though there is much that may be learned about man from the natural and social sciences, man himself in his inmost being as a person can never be comprehended by these means.

Nevertheless, unlike some of the existentialists (for example, Karl Jaspers), Bultmann has never been led by this insight to repudiate the possibility of some kind of a scientific analysis of man's inner or personal life. On the contrary, he has accepted the view of Martin Heidegger that a science of man

---

[69] *Kerygma und Mythos*, I, p. 24 (p. 12). Cf. *Glauben and Verstehen*, I, pp. 262 f., 315, 331; also *Kerygma und Mythos*, II, pp. 184 f., and *Jesus Christ and Mythology*, p. 18.

as an existing self is possible and that it is one of the tasks of the philosopher to work out such an "existential analysis." Thus, he refers in one place to "a science that speaks of existence [*sic* man] without objectifying it to worldly being."[70] He points out that such a science is possible because there is always an understanding of existence already more or less clearly given with existence itself. Man not only exists in the sense we shall presently define; he also understands he exists, or, as Heidegger puts it, he is "disclosed" (*erschlossen*) to himself as existing.[71] Consequently, there not only can be sciences that speak of man as an object in the world, but there can be "a science that is nothing more than the clear and methodical explication of the understanding of existence given with existence itself."[72]

Bultmann believes that just such a science has been attempted with evident success in Heidegger's phenomenological analysis of human existence in *Sein und Zeit*. Although he recognises that conclusive knowledge is no more to be had in this area than in any other, he has an extraordinarily high regard for Heidegger's scientific accomplishment.[73] Indeed, as John Macquarrie has beautifully shown, the ontology of human existence that Bultmann presupposes in almost all his theological work is precisely the one developed by the early Heidegger.

[70] *Kerygma und Mythos*, II, p. 187.

[71] Cf. Martin Heidegger, *Sein und Zeit*, Vol. I, Tübingen: Neomarius Verlag, 6th ed., 1949, pp. 130-134.

[72] *Kerygma und Mythos*, II, p. 189. Cf. pp. 192 f. (p. 193). We may note that Bultmann fails consistently to maintain this distinction between an " objectifying " and a " non-objectifying " science of man. In places, he allows that existential analysis also has an " objective " character. Cf. his reply to Karl Jaspers in H. W. Bartsch (ed.), *Kerygma und Mythos*, Vol. III, Hamburg: Herbert Reich-Evangelischer Verlag, 1954, p. 54 (English translation in Karl Jaspers and Rudolf Bultmann, *Myth and Christianity*, New York: The Noonday Press, 1958, pp. 64 f.); cf. also *Glauben und Verstehen*, Vol. III, Tübingen: J. C. B. Mohr, 1960, pp. 107-121.

[73] Bultmann's most explicit statement of his relation to Heidegger is given in the essay " The Historicity of Man and Faith," *Existence and Faith*, pp. 92-110.

If, then, one is to understand Bultmann's work, he must first understand Heidegger's existential analysis. For our purpose, however, such understanding must be assumed, and we must focus our attention directly on the way in which Bultmann himself makes use of the ontological concept of "existence."

In the reply to his critics in the second volume of *Kerygma und Mythos*, Bultmann writes that the "right" philosophy "does not raise the question of the meaning of existence as an *existentiell* question, but, knowing that such a question can be answered only in the act of existing itself, inquires about the meaning of existence in general." Thus, philosophy shows man "what existence means. It shows him that human being, as distinguished from all other being, means to exist, to be a being given over to itself, which has to assume responsibility for itself. It shows him that his existence is authentic only in the act of existing and therefore realises itself only in the moment, in the concrete here and now. Philosophy does not intend by its existential analysis, however, to create an *existentiell* understanding of the here and now. It does not relieve man of this responsibility, but rather assigns it precisely to him."[74] In addition to clarifying the function of philosophy as Bultmann usually speaks of it, these sentences point up three defining characteristics of the concept of "existence."

In the first place, they make clear that "existence" refers to a specific type of being, which is distinguished from other types by having a relation to itself. Unlike the animal, which is "indifferent" towards its being, man is inveterately concerned with his existence. What he is, is never simply given, as in the case of inanimate objects or other subhuman creatures, but, rather, is always in question and must be responsibly laid hold of by free decision. Heidegger expresses this by saying that man's being is a "possibility of being" (*Seinkönnen*), or,

[74] *Kerygma und Mythos*, II, pp. 192 f. (pp. 193 f.). Cf. *Jesus Christ and Mythology*, pp. 55 ff.

still more graphically, that *"Dasein [sic* man] *is* his possibility."[75] Heidegger's point is that man not only *has* possibilities, like everything else, but actually *is* a possibility for which he himself continually has to decide. Man lives only by moving beyond himself and projecting himself into his own freely chosen possibility of existence. Consciously or unconsciously, he is always moved by the question of who he ought to be and in his individual decisions in the moment is constantly giving an answer to this *existentiell* question.

This suggests the second characteristic of "existence" that is illumined by Bultmann's statement. If man is the being who is related to himself and therefore responsible for himself, his being is always his own individual being. Heidegger writes: "The being with which this reality [*sic Dasein*] is concerned is my own particular being [*je meines Sein*]. Therefore, *Dasein* is never to be understood ontologically as an instance or exemplar of some species of merely extant things. . . . When [it] speaks it must, in accordance with its characteristic of *Jemeinigkeit*, constantly use the personal pronouns, 'I am,' 'You are.' "[76] What Heidegger speaks of here as *Jemeinigkeit* is the very thing Bultmann expresses when he says that only in the act of existing itself can the *existentiell* question be answered. Only the individual man in his own unique existence can decide who he is to be.

The third characteristic of "existence" is conveyed by the phrase "an *existentiell* understanding of the here and now." Bultmann argues that a sharp distinction must be made between the *existential* or philosophical understanding of existence in general and the *existentiell* understanding that the individual always has of his own unique situation. Whereas for the former, the object of understanding is the phenomenon of existence as such, for the latter, it is the individual person in one of his possible ways of existing. The latter kind of understanding must be taken into account because the act of existing

[75] *Ob. cit.*, p. 42.   [76] *Ibid.*

whereby the individual decides who he is to be is simultaneously an act of understanding, or, as may also be said, "self-understanding" (*Selbstverständnis*). In Heidegger's words, a "*Desein* is the reality that in its being understandingly relates itself to this being. To say this is to define the formal concept of *Existenz*."[77] In other words, to exist and to have an understanding of oneself in relation to others and the world are one and the same thing, for the answer to the *existentiell* question of who one is to be always takes the form of just such a self-understanding.

This does not mean, as Bultmann has frequently pointed out, that such understanding is necessarily conscious. On the contrary, it frequently is not. The point, however, is that even when we are not consciously aware of it, we are continually moved by the *existentiell* question of the meaning of our existence, and are constantly giving an answer to it by the way in which we understand ourselves.[78] We may also point out that "*existentiell* understanding" is incorrectly understood so long as it is thought to refer to something purely intellectual or theoretical. Although the existential understanding practised in philosophical analysis *is* theoretical, the understanding each of us has of himself in the concrete moment is not theoretical but *practical*. It is a type of understanding that places a value on what is understood and so is meaningful only insofar as it is continually reaffirmed by personal decision. It has an inescapable imperative meaning, to overlook which by regarding it as something purely indicative (as has been done, for example, by Helmut Thielicke) is to misunderstand it.[79]

For man to "exist," in the technical sense that Bultmann presupposes, means he is a being who must continually face

---

[77] *Ibid.*, p. 53.

[78] Cf. *Kerygma und Mythos*, ii, p. 201 (p. 203); also *Jesus Christ and Mythology*, pp. 74 f.

[79] Cf. *Kerygma und Mythos*, ii, p. 201 (pp. 202 f.). Cf. also Thielicke's essay in *Kerygma und Mythos*, i, pp. 165 f. (pp. 146 f.).

and answer the question of what it is to be a man. It means, in a word, that he is *a moral or religious being*, one who always has to deal with the problem of what he *ought* to be. What he is to be is never already determined, but, rather, is something he himself is required to decide freely and responsibly by his *existentiell* understanding of himself in his world.

The mention of "world" introduces yet a further characteristic of the concept "existence" that must be clarified. According to Heidegger, what is disclosed to man by the understanding of himself given with his existence is not just that he exists, but that his being is a "being-in-the-world" (*In-der-Welt-Sein*).[80] In this instance, "in" does not have the meaning of spatial inclusion, but, rather, denotes a uniquely existential relationship that may be comprehensively described as "concern" (*Besorgen*). For *man* to be in the world means such different things as for him to have to do with something, to produce something, to lose something, to ask for something, to observe something—where "something" in each case refers to an object of his concern, and so to what Heidegger means by "world."[81] Accordingly, *things* are "in" the world in the sense of being within someone's field of existential concern, or, in different terms, the world-structure within which the various objects in the world find their places is ontologically prior to the objects themselves.[82] Our first awareness of things does not regard them as mere objects of knowledge, but as tools or instruments for implementing our basic *existentiell* projects. As Heidegger puts it, the things with which we are confronted are, first of all, "at hand" (*zuhanden*) rather than "on hand" (*vorhanden*); they are not laid out for disinterested observation, but are available to us as means for realising our individual understandings of what it means to be human.[83] Even so, we may recall from our earlier discussion that this primitive "work-thinking," as Bultmann speaks of it, implicitly

[80] *Op. cit.*, p. 55; also pp. 132 f. [81] *Ibid.*, pp. 53-57. [82] *Ibid.*, pp. 72-76. [83] *Ibid.*, pp. 68 ff.

contains what may subsequently become science. Objective thinking may at any time be released from narrow bondage to practical concern and develop into what we should recognise as scientific thought. Nevertheless, the existence of applied science and technology serves to remind us of the ultimate practical basis and consequences of even the most disinterested research.

The importance of the concept "world" for our present purpose is that it enables us to understand that, in addition to being someone who is concerned with answering the *existentiell* question, man is also characterised by constantly giving answers to a second and different type of question. From an epistemological standpoint, for man to be in the world means that he possesses a more or less complex and integrated system of objective statements or answers to the question "What is?" This may also be expressed by saying that the contents of the "world," inclusive of both its "facts" and its "principles," are defined by the total number of "is-assertions" that the individual subject is able to make on the basis of his experience.[84] Even where these assertions are still closely bound to immediate practical concerns (where a tree, for example, is still only something to be hollowed out to make a boat) or are made uncritically, to be in a position to make them is what it means to be in the world.

To say, then, with Heidegger and Bultmann, that man is disclosed to himself as existing in the world is to say that he is revealed as having both practical (or *existentiell*) and theoretical functions. He is disclosed to himself not only as a moral or religious being who must continually deal with the *existentiell* question of who he ought to be, but also as a being who is constantly answering the question "What is?" by making objective statements about his world.

But if this is true, it would seem to follow that the various forms of human expression or communication finally serve one

---

[84] Cf. *Glauben und Verstehen*, I, pp. 154 f.

or the other of two basic purposes. And, this, indeed, is the implication Bultmann everywhere presupposes. Throughout his writings he assumes that what is presented in any written document (or, for that matter, any instance of oral communication) is either (1) objective statements that provide information about the world and the phenomena within it, or (2) *existentiell* statements through which the reader (or hearer) is confronted with a decision about his possibilities of self-understanding. Bultmann explicitly clarifies this assumption in the context of his hermeneutics, or general theory of historical understanding. It is to this theory we must now turn in order to understand his project of existential interpretation.

In the systematic statement in the essay, "Das Problem der Hermeneutik,"[85] Bultmann begins by accepting the thesis of Wilhelm Dilthey that hermeneutics is "the science of the understanding of history in general."[86] As such, he goes on to argue, it is concerned with such questions as whether an objectively valid understanding of history is possible and, if so, what the conditions are under which it may be achieved. In the course of a brief but perceptive survey of the previous discussion of these questions, especially as it developed in the period after Schleiermacher, Bultmann sets forth his own answers. He elaborates a general theory of the interpretation of literary texts that takes the form of two basic theses.

First of all, he affirms that all interpretation of written documents must take place in accordance with certain "hermeneutical rules" gradually worked out through the continuing discussion of the problem of historical understanding. Thus, for example, it is necessary to interpret a text on the basis of a formal analysis of its structure and style. The

---

[85] *Glauben und Verstehen*, II, pp. 211-235 (pp. 234-261). Cf. the parallel statements in *The Presence of Eternity: History and Eschatology*, New York: Harper & Brothers, 1957, pp. 110-122; *Existence and Faith*, pp. 289-296; *Jesus Christ and Mythology*, pp. 45-59; *Glauben und Verstehen*, III, pp. 109 ff.

[86] *Ibid.*, p. 212 (p. 235).

interpreter is required to analyse the composition of the work and to understand its parts in terms of the whole, and the whole, again, in terms of its parts. Similarly, he must interpret the work in accordance with grammar and with a knowledge of the writer's peculiar linguistic usage. To these three rules, which were already formulated even in the ancient world, scholars of the Enlightenment added the further requirement for a knowledge of the linguistic usage of the epoch in which the text was written and of its more general historical conditions.[87] Bultmann has pointed out in a more recent essay that these "hermeneutical rules" together constitute "the historical method of interrogating a text," which in turn "includes the presupposition that history is a unity in the sense of a closed continuum . . . in which individual events are connected by the succession of cause and effect."[88]

Bultmann's second thesis is that the more fundamental "presupposition" for interpreting a document is that the interpreter have a "life-relation" to what the document expresses. "The presupposition of every understanding interpretation is *a previous life-relation to the subject matter [Sache]* that is directly or indirectly expressed in the text and constitutes the object [*Woraufhin*] of the inquiry. Without such a relation in which text and interpreter are bound together, inquiry and understanding are impossible and inquiry is not even motivated."[89] This point is further clarified in another passage : "The condition of interpretation is that the interpreter and the author are both men and live in the same historical world in which human existence takes place as existence in an environment, in understanding intercourse with objects and fellow-men."[90] In other words, the attempt to understand a historical document presupposes that the interpreter already shares, at least in principle, the experiences the document represents. Bultmann frequently expresses this

---

[87] *Ibid.*, pp. 212 f. (pp. 235 f.). [88] *Existence and Faith*, p. 291.
[89] *Glauben und Verstehen*, ii, p. 227 (p. 252). [90] *Ibid.*, p. 219 (p. 243).

by saying that every interpretation must be guided by a "pre-understanding" (*Vorverständnis*) of the subject matter of which a text directly or indirectly speaks.[91] Unless in some sense or other the interpreter already understands what a text expresses, it is impossible for him to understand it at all. What is more, his attempt to interpret the text is, as Bultmann says, completely unmotivated; for, in the final analysis, the only things about which he wishes to ask are those he in some way already knows.

It is at this point in Bultmann's argument that his basic view of man begins to be determinative. For though he gives several examples of the way in which man's various "life-relations" establish different "preunderstandings," and so give rise to different ways of putting questions to historical texts, he finally acknowledges only two basic approaches to historical understanding.[92] In accordance with his general view of man and of the forms of human expression, he takes for granted that any attempt to understand a text takes place in terms of one or the other of two fundamental questions: "What is?" or "What ought to be?"

In the former case, what understanding presupposes is that the author of the text and the interpreter live in the same world and that the things or processes described by the former's "is-assertions" or objective statements are also accessible to the latter—if not in fact, then in principle. Thus, in order for me to understand a description of the coiffure of ancient Egyptian women or a narrative of Jackson's attack on the second day at Chancellorsville, it is necessary that I have a "life-relation" to such things as feminine hair styles and military tactics.[93]

A parallel condition holds good for the second type of under-

[91] Cf., e.g., *ibid.*, p. 227 (p. 252). Cf. also *Existence and Faith*, pp. 292-295.

[92] Cf. especially the essay, " Wissenschaft und Existenz " (*Glauben und Verstehen*, III, pp. 107-121), the title of which alone is sufficient indication this is so.

[93] Cf. *Glauben und Verstehen*, II, pp. 218 ff. (pp. 242 ff.); also *Glauben und Verstehen*, I, p. 125.

standing. The only reason I can understand a text that directly or indirectly speaks to me of my existence is because I already have an understanding relation to myself and to my different *existentiell* possibilities. "Every historical understanding assumes that the subject matter to be interpreted belongs to my existence, that my existence has the character of being disclosed to itself [*Erschlossenheit*], that I more or less clearly know about my possibilities. I can evade this knowledge, I can hide it from myself, I can forget it; but I have it. . . . Without asking, I cannot hear. . . . But in order to be able to ask, I must in a certain sense already know."[94]

What Bultmann means by "existential interpretation" is this second type of historical understanding. It is an interpretation that rests on man's preunderstanding of his own *existentiell* possibilities and therefore is oriented in terms of the question "What ought to be?" According to the argument in "Das Problem der Hermeneutik," such interpretation is especially appropriate to works in the areas of philosophy and religion and what may be called serious literature.[95] What is presented in each of these forms of expression is some attempt to speak to the *existentiell* question of the meaning of man's existence.

The intention of a serious novelist or dramatist, for example, is not simply to present objective statements and so describe events and processes in the world, but rather to appeal to the reader's or viewer's self-understanding by confronting him with some of his possibilities for understanding his existence.[96] The same thing is pre-eminently true of philosophical and religious documents. To regard a philosophical system as just so many objective "doctrines" or as a stage in the past discussion of certain speculative questions is to misunderstand it. The philosopher's purpose is to speak a living word to the

[94] *Glauben und Verstehen*, I, p. 128.
[95] Cf. *Glauben und Verstehen*, II, p. 228 (p. 253).
[96] Cf. *ibid.*, p. 221 (pp. 245 f.).

present by calling all who hear his voice to a radical reflection about the meaning of their existence. Hence the appropriate question to put to his work is the *existentiell* question.[97]

This is even truer of works in the area of religion. According to Bultmann, religious documents especially intend to give an answer to the *existentiell* question.[98] We recall from the preceding section that it is on this basis that he proposes to interpret myth. Myth should be understood, he claims, not in terms of its objective contents, but in terms of the understanding of human existence these contents inadequately express. Although Bultmann does not mean by this that the original users of myth failed to reckon realistically with its objective meaning, and self-consciously employed it to express their self-understanding, still the actual meaning of myth is to be found in its answer to the *existentiell* question. Thus, for example, throughout all the variety and inconsistency of the myths of Gnosticism, there runs the theme of a single understanding of human existence.[99] Similarly, the Old Testament-Jewish idea of creation is incorrectly understood as long as it is regarded cosmologically as a narrative about an extraordinary event at the beginning of time. The statement that God is the Creator is "in its fundamental intention not the statement of a cosmological theory that seeks to explain the origin of the world, but rather man's confession to God as his Lord—the Lord to whom the world belongs, whose power

[97] Cf. *ibid.*, p. 222 (p. 246). Cf. also *Glauben und Verstehen*, III, p. 122 (English translation by H. O. J. Brown in Walter Leibrecht [ed.], *Religion and Culture: Essays in Honor of Paul Tillich*, New York: Harper & Brothers, 1959, p. 236). We may simply note at this point, pending further discussion in Sec. 5, the obvious tension between the view of philosophy presupposed here and the conception of it as a purely formal ontological analysis referred to earlier in the section.

[98] Cf. the Introduction to *Das Urchristentum im Rahmen der antiken Religionen*, Zürich: Artemis-Verlag, 1949, pp. 7 f. (English translation by R. H. Fuller in Rudolf Bultmann, *Primitive Christianity in Its Contemporary Setting*, New York: Meridian Books, Inc., 1956, pp. 11 f.).

[99] Cf. *ibid.*, pp. 181 ff. (pp. 162 ff.).

and care sustain and preserve it, and to whom man himself owes obedience."[100]

Whether a work be literary, philosophical, or religious, it basically intends to express some understanding of the meaning of human existence. Accordingly, Bultmann argues, the question with which one must approach it is not, first of all, the theoretical or objective question "What is ?" but the practical or *existentiell* question "What ought to be ?" In short, what is required is "existential interpretation."

The reference above to Bultmann's interpretation of the Old Testament idea of creation suggests that he applies these same procedures of historical understanding to the exegesis of Holy Scripture. Despite his concern to move beyond the historicism of the nineteenth century by developing an exegetical method that can more appropriately deal with the biblical writings, he has consistently opposed all proposals for a special "theological" or "pneumatic" exegesis.[101] In his view, the only proper approach to interpreting Scripture is the same approach required for interpreting any other document of the same basic type. Thus he writes : "The interpretation of the biblical writings is subject to no different conditions of understanding than hold good for any other piece of literature."[102] But this means that (1) understanding of the Scriptures must be governed by the several hermeneutical rules that together constitute the historical method of interrogating a text, and (2) "the presupposition for understanding here also is the bond between the text and the interpreter

---

[100] *Ibid.*, p. 11; cf. p. 14 (p. 15; cf. p. 18). Cf. *Existence and Faith*, pp. 206ff.

[101] Cf. " Das Problem einer theologischen Exegese des Neuen Testaments," *Zwischen den Zeiten*, 4. Heft, 1925, pp. 356 f.; also *Glauben und Verstehen*, I, pp. 127 f. and 132 f.; *Glauben und Verstehen*, II, p. 212, n. 4 (pp. 235, n. 2); and *Kerygma und Mythos*, II, pp. 191 f. (p. 192). The contrary claim of John Otwell in " Neo-Orthodoxy and Biblical Research," *Harvard Theological Review*, April, 1950, pp. 145-157, is completely incorrect.

[102] *Glauben und Verstehen*, II, p. 231 (p. 256). Cf. *Existence and Faith*, pp. 292 and 295 f.

provided by the latter's life-relation or previous connection with the subject matter the former seeks to relate."[103]

This second condition has been hotly contested by some of Bultmann's critics.[104] To speak of the necessity for a "pre-understanding" of the kerygma has seemed to them dangerously to compromise the Reformers' principle of *sola scriptura—sola gratia*. Nevertheless, Bultmann has continued to insist that "here, too, the presupposition for understanding is a pre-understanding of the subject matter to be understood."[105]

> . . . if it is objected that man cannot know who God is and therefore also cannot know what an act of God means before God has revealed himself, then it is to be replied that *man can very well know who God is in the question concerning him.* If man's existence were not moved (consciously or unconsciously) by the question concerning God in the sense of Augustine's *"Tu nos fecisti ad Te, et cor nostrum inquietum est, donec requiescat in Te,"* he would not be able to recognise God in any revelation. There is an *existentiell* knowledge of God at work in human existence in the question concerning "happiness" or "salvation," or the meaning of the world and of history—or, in short, in the question concerning the authenticity [*Eigentlichkeit*] of one's own existence.[106]

Bultmann does concede that the right to speak of the *existentiell* question as "the question concerning God" is given only to faith ; but he in no way intends this to qualify the claim that "the phenomenon itself [*sic* the *existentiell* question] constitutes a relation to the subject matter of revelation."[107]

The kind of interpretation that Bultmann proposes to apply to the New Testament is the kind appropriate for any other work of serious literature, philosophy, or religion. He

---

[103] *Ibid.*
[104] Cf., e.g., *Existence and Faith*, pp. 99-102.
[105] *Glauben und Verstehen*, II, p. 231 (p. 256).
[106] *Ibid.*, pp. 231 f. (p. 257). Cf. *Jesus Christ and Mythology*, pp. 52 f.
[107] *Glauben und Verstehen*, II, p. 232 (pp. 257 f.).

believes that only when the New Testament is approached in this way is it possible to do justice to its primary intention to speak to the question of man's existence.

He further believes that when the New Testament is approached existentially there is the possibility of an adequate solution to the problem posed by its mythological form of expression. For in his judgment, myth is by no means the only "conceptuality" (*Begrifflichkeit*) in which it is possible to speak of human existence. "The anxiety about demythologisation," he writes, "may be based in part on the unexamined presupposition that there is an either/or between mythology and a science that can speak of existence only by objectifying it to worldly being. But is there no other language than that of science and myth ? Are statements like 'I love you' or 'I beg your pardon' spoken in scientific language ? If not, is the language in which they are expressed mythological ? Indeed, there is *a language in which existence naïvely expresses itself*, and, corresponding to this language, there is also *a science that speaks of existence without objectifying it to worldly being*."[108] In other words, as a result of the labours of modern philosophers, there is also a non-mythological conceptuality in which one may speak of man and his various *existentiell* possibilities.

This is what Bultmann has in mind when he speaks of Heidegger's existential analysis as "the 'right' philosophy."[109] Heidegger's analysis is "right" in the sense that it offers a precise conceptuality in which the phenomena of human existence may be appropriately described in a non-mythological way.[110] If the New Testament message is an *existentiell*

---

[108] *Kerygma und Mythos*, II, p. 187.

[109] Cf. *ibid.*, pp. 192 ff. (pp. 192 ff.); also *Jesus Christ and Mythology*, pp. 54 ff.

[110] Cf. *Kerygma und Mythos*, I, p. 124 (p. 104); also *Existence and Faith*, pp. 288 and 92-110. If this point is understood, it is impossible to say with Macquarrie that, in describing Bultmann's project, "it would be more accurate to speak of transmythologisation than of demythologisation" (*op. cit.*, p. 176). Macquarrie is here betrayed by his own "wider" definition of myth and fails

communication that summons man to a certain self-understanding, there not only is the possibility of restating it in a demythologised form, but there is also the possibility that in the process it will finally be brought to an adequate expression. The exegete has available to him concepts in which the New Testament's intention to speak to man's existence may be realised without the impediments of a mythological form of expression. Therefore, the task of interpretation, which begins with the historical and philological work prescribed by the hermeneutical rules, may be brought to its proper completion in an understandable translation of the New Testament mythology.

What are the characteristics of such a translation? What sort of a restatement of the kerygma does Bultmann present when he approaches it with the *existentiell* question and the non-mythological conceptuality of Heidegger's existential analysis?

It could be inferred from the previous discussion that the logical form of such a statement would be an exposition of "the Christian understanding of existence." And this, indeed, is the very form followed by Bultmann himself in the systematic summary in Part II of "Neues Testament und Mythologie."[111] Since for our purpose the important point is the logical structure of Bultmann's thought, this same form seems most appropriate for our own exposition.

Before we begin the exposition, some general comments may help to explain its rationale.

Because in the nature of the case, to answer the question "What ought to be?" is also to decide the question "What ought not to be?" an existential interpretation is complete only when it has set forth the answer to this second question

---

to see that, in *Bultmann's sense of the word*, Heidegger's existential conceptuality is not at all mythological.

[111] Cf. pp. 27-31 (pp. 17-22).

given in the text to be interpreted. In the case of the New Testament, this is relatively easy to do, since it is polemical throughout and carries on its discussion of the good life only by explicitly contrasting the latter with what life ought not to be. Since, moreover, the self-understanding in which the New Testament locates the good is what it calls "faith," an exposition of its view of man's two basic possibilities naturally follows the pattern of presenting human existence as it takes place "in" faith and as it takes place "outside" it. Because, however, faith is not a possibility open to "the natural man," but rather is contingent on God's eschatological act in Christ, it is only appropriate to consider life outside faith before considering the new understanding of faith itself. Bultmann also points out that the portrait of the natural man presented in the New Testament depicts him not as he appears to himself, but as he appears from the subsequent standpoint of faith. In Bultmann's peculiar terminology, the proper task of "a legitimate natural theology" (that is, a natural theology carried out by faith itself) is to portray the existence of the natural man in this way.[112]

What, then, are the features of this portrait?

According to Bultmann, the New Testament's view bears a strong resemblance to the understanding of man's situation implied in the Gnostic myth of redemption. The New Testament not only uses the conceptuality of Gnosticism in characterising existence outside faith, but even shares the Gnostic view that man's destiny in the world is one of fallenness into bondage under inimical cosmic powers.[113]

Even so, there is a fundamental difference between the two understandings of existence. For the New Testament, man's destiny is not, as in Gnosticism, the result of a cosmic fate, but the consequence of his own free and responsible decision.

---

[112] Cf. *Existence and Faith*, p. 305, n. 19; cf. also *Glauben und Verstehen*, I, pp. 311 f.

[113] Cf. *Kerygma und Mythos*, I, p. 27 (p. 17).

This is made clear by the fact that the New Testament everywhere rejects the Gnostic idea of the pre-existence of the human self and, refusing to surrender the Old Testament faith in God as the Creator, transforms Gnosticism's cosmological dualism into a dualism of decision.[114] An even clearer indication is the way in which Paul immediately qualifies his statement that through Adam sin and death have come unto the world by saying that death spread to all men "because *all* men sinned" (Rom. 5 : 12). Likewise, Paul elsewhere traces mankind's plight not to Adam's fall, but to men's failure to acknowledge the God whose eternal power and deity are visible in the things that have been made (Rom. 1 : 18 ff.).[115]

Thus, the New Testament's emphasis on man's freedom and responsibility sharply distinguishes its view from that of Gnosticism. However much it may use the latter's concepts and, indeed, even picture man's situation naturalistically as fate rather than as freedom, it never forgets that man is an existing self or person who must bear the responsibility for his plight.

This is further borne out by the way in which Paul speaks of "flesh." As he uses the term, it does not mean man's sensual nature, which is continually getting the best of his reason, but refers to the entire sphere of what is objectively visible and manageable, which comes to determine man's existence only when he himself freely decides to live "according" to it.[116] In other words, it is not "flesh" that controls man, at least not at first, but it is man himself, his desire to find and secure his existence, that first gives the things of "flesh" their fateful power over him. Only because he tries to find his existence in the creature rather than in the Creator is "the world" transformed into "this world" and he himself delivered into bondage to it. Here, too, it is clear that the only

[114] Cf. *Theologie des Neuen Testaments*, pp. 367-373 and 392 f. (II, pp. 15-21 and 40).

[115] Cf. *Das Urchristentum*, p. 213 (p. 191).

[116] Cf. *ibid.*, p. 214 (p. 192); also *Kerygma und Mythos*, I, p. 28 (p. 18).

fate of which the New Testament speaks is a fate that is simultaneously guilt.[117]

The final consequence of life "according to the flesh" is death. "Because man understands himself in terms of what he accomplishes and produces, because he thus takes his god-*less* being to be his authentic, his ultimate being, he is punished by death's—i.e., the death to which the whole of his present existence is subject—also acquiring for him the character of something authentic and ultimate."[118] In this sense, we may understand the New Testament's mythological assertions that death came into the world through sin and that "the wages of sin is death" (Rom. 5 : 12 ; 6 : 23).

An even more terrifying consequence of man's attempt to secure his life is what happens to his relationship with his fellow-men. The dependence on transitory things into which he falls as soon as he makes "flesh" the measure of his life inevitably finds expression in an attitude of lovelessness towards his neighbour. In his anxious concern to secure his existence, each pursues his own interests in getting and having with an utter disregard for the needs of the other person. Only a mutual desire for security and protection against the encroachments of others leads to a mitigation of a *bellum omnium contra omnes* and gives rise to certain minimum standards of justice and right. According to Bultmann, it is this general atmosphere of self-seeking and hatred, relieved only by a morality of contract and convention, that is primarily connoted by the Fourth Gospel's concept of "the world."[119] In John's sense, to be "of the world" means, on the one hand, to be governed in all of one's actions by just such an attitude of lovelessness (cf. 15 : 19) and, on the other hand, to be bound in all of one's judgments by certain conventional standards and values (cf. 5 : 41 ff. ; 6 : 41 f. ; 7 : 27, 52). Although it is each man's heritage in being born to enter a "world" in this sense of the

---

[117] Cf. *Das Urchristentum*, pp. 213 f. (pp. 191 f.).
[118] *Existence and Faith*, p. 82.   [119] Cf. *Glauben und Verstehen*, I, p. 135, n. 3.

word, still it is only when he himself surrenders his freedom by seeking to become his own master that he too becomes loveless, and the world's standards and judgments also come to dominate his thought and action. Thus "the world is reconstituted [*mitkonstituiert*] by each individual and as such becomes a power over him. It becomes the destiny he himself has created."[120]

This, then, is the portrait presented by the New Testament's mythological statements concerning the natural man. When it speaks of man in the concepts of Gnosticism as existing in bondage to cosmic powers, what it really wants to say, as becomes evident from the critical way in which it makes use of its concepts, is that human existence outside of faith is (to use Heidegger's terminology) "inauthentic" (*uneigentlich*) existence. Therefore, Bultmann feels completely justified in translating the mythological concepts in the general manner outlined in the preceding paragraphs. He holds that it is just when these concepts are replaced by existential ones (that is, concepts explicitly portraying man as an existing self who is free and responsible) that the New Testament's own understanding of existence outside of faith can be appropriately expressed.

Bultmann further holds that the translation thus provided can be understood by modern men in a way in which the New Testament's original formulations cannot. When the life of the natural man is presented not as an enslavement under mythical powers, but as an inauthentic self-understanding, the barrier posed by a mythological conceptuality is removed.

Similar conclusions may also be drawn concerning the New Testament's understanding of the life of faith. If every self-understanding that locates man's good in something that can be objectively seen and managed is what ought *not* to be, what *ought* to be is an understanding of one's existence in

[120] *Das Urchristentum*, p. 216 (p. 193).

which the end of life is found in what is invisible and unmanageable. According to Bultmann, it is just such an *existentiell* attitude of openness to the future that the New Testament myths intend to express in speaking of life "according to the Spirit" or "in faith."[121]

Such a life out of the invisible is possible as faith in God's grace, that is, the confidence that the unknown and unmanageable transcendent confronts man as a holy love which gives him his future and so releases him from his past. In this sense, it is life under the forgiveness of sin; for what the New Testament means by "sin" is the lack of confidence or anxiety at the bottom of the natural man's self-understanding, which betrays him into his bondage to the past.[122] So long as man refuses to trust God and seeks instead to find his life in the world, his being becomes pure past, and any future he may think he has is an illusion. "In every actual choice in which man chooses a possibility of existing authentically he in fact always chooses what he already is . . . he never gets rid of his past and therefore is never free."[123] In "faith," however, this bondage to the past is broken. Because man then looks solely to God for his security and trusts completely in him, all the motives that previously controlled his action are deprived of their determinative power. This means that faith is also "obedience" (cf. Rom. 1 : 5). For such an absolute trust in God is nothing less than the surrender of all of one's self-contrived securities and the renunciation of every attempt to acquire and maintain one's life (cf. Phil. 3 : 17 ff.).

This is all well expressed in the New Testament's claim that the life of faith is a life of radical "freedom." In its negative aspect, such freedom is "freedom *from* the world" (*Entweltlichung*), from the whole sphere of what is objectively visible and controllable. As such, however, it must be sharply

---

[121] Cf. *ibid.*, p. 205 (p. 184); also *Kerygma und Mythos*, 1, p. 29 (p. 19).
[122] Cf. especially *Glauben und Verstehen*, 11, p. 71 (p. 81).
[123] *Existence and Faith*, p. 107.

distinguished from all forms of asceticism. What is meant by the Christian's freedom from the world is not the dualist's devaluation of "sense" or "matter," but rather an attitude of inner distance from *all* worldly attachments. It is the dialectical attitude of "as though not" that Paul enjoins in I Corinthians 7 : 29-31.

But Christian freedom is not simply negative. At the same time that it is a freedom *from*, it is also a freedom *for*. Paul, for example, no sooner boasts of his freedom from all men than he adds : "I have made myself a slave to all" (I Cor. 9 : 19). This slavery of service, or "love," is the positive aspect of the Christian man's freedom.[124] Since his freedom from the world is simultaneously a freedom for God, it is also a freedom for God's concrete demand as it encounters him in the person of his neighbour. Thus the "obedience" of faith has a further meaning : To obey God is to obey his commandments that point one to his fellow-man (cf. I John 4 : 20 ; Gal. 5 : 6 ; Rom, 13 : 8 ff.).

To exist in this way, in freedom from the past and openness for the future, is what the New Testament understands by "eschatological existence." When Paul speaks of being a "new creation" (II Cor. 5 : 17), or John, of having passed from death to "eternal life" (cf. John 5 : 24), they mean precisely this kind of an *existentiell* self-understanding (cf. Gal. 5 : 6 and I Cor. 7 : 19 with Gal. 6 : 15). This is evident from the fact that what distinguishes the New Testament from Jewish apocalypticism is its conviction that the time of salvation has already broken in and the life of the world to come is even now a reality for those who believe.[125] Although the implications of this conviction are radically developed only in the theologies of Paul and John, especially the latter, even in the earliest community, in its understanding of itself as the already-present eschatological congregation, the way is prepared for a

[124] Cf. *ibid.*, p. 85.
[125] Cf. *Kerygma und Mythos*, 1, p. 30 (p. 20).

demythologisation of apocalyptic eschatology.[126] For the New Testament writers, the decisive eschatological occurrence is not an imminent cosmic catastrophe, but the fact that God is now judging the world in Jesus Christ and thereby calling men to decide for life or death (cf. John 3 : 19 ; 9 : 39).

Even so, the New Testament's eschatology is not to be identified with that of Gnosticism. Though it shares the Gnostic view that man's true life is even now a reality, it does not hold that this life consists in the emancipation of a pre-existent "nature" or that man's final destiny is already guaranteed. "Life in faith is not a condition that may be unambiguously described by the indicative. On the contrary, it is such that the imperative also is required to describe it. That is, the decision of faith is not made once and for all, but must be reaffirmed in each concrete situation by being made anew."[127] For this reason, the New Testament knows virtually nothing of the libertinism and asceticism so characteristic of Gnostic spirituality. The believer's freedom does not exempt him from the moral demand, but, rather, is expressed precisely in obedience to it (cf. Rom. 6 : 11 ff.). On the other hand, such obedience takes a different form from the Gnostic's anxious asceticism.

The decisive evidence for the New Testament's rejection of Gnostic views, however, can be seen in Paul's notion of "the Spirit." However much Paul may think of the Spirit as a mysterious power that can be possessed and so guarantee one's resurrection (cf. Rom. 8 : 11), "it is clear that he basically understands by 'Spirit' the factual possibility of a new life, which is opened up in faith. The 'Spirit' does not operate as a natural force, nor does it really become the possession of the believer. Rather, it is the factual possibility of life that must be laid hold of by decision."[128] Hence we may under-

---

[126] Cf. *Kerygma und Mythos*, ii, p. 205 (p. 208); also *Theologie des Neuen Testaments*, pp. 39 and 45 ff. (i, pp. 36 f. and 42 ff.).

[127] *Kerygma und Mythos*, i, p. 30 (p. 20). [128] *Ibid.*, p. 31 (p. 22).

stand Paul's paradoxical exhortation in Galatians 5 : 25 : "If we live by the Spirit, then let us also walk by the Spirit" (cf. also Rom. 6 : 13). Just as living "according to the flesh" is not a condition of "nature," but a certain possibility of historical existence, so also life "according to the Spirit" is not a new supernatural state, but a possible way of existing as a self that must constantly be decided for anew.

Finally, we may mention Paul's doctrine of the sacraments. Although he continually employs the sacramental conceptions of the mystery religions (cf. Rom. 6 : 3 ff. and I Cor. 10 : 16 f.) and even shares their view that the sacraments have a quasi-physical power (I Cor. 11 : 29 f.), he nevertheless rejects the idea that the sacraments afford any guarantee of salvation (cf. I Cor. 10 : 1-13 ; 11 : 27-29 ; 1 : 17). In his view, it is not because of the elements that the sacraments are effective, but because or insofar as the grace they make available is obediently received in faith. Thus "the life bestowed by the sacraments stands just as much under the imperative as under the indicative."[129]

In sum, what the New Testament speaks of mythologically as life in faith may be appropriately translated by Heidegger's concept of "authentic" (*eigentlich*) historical existence. Bultmann believes this conclusion is unavoidable if one attends carefully to the way in which the New Testament utilises its mythological concepts. Whether one considers Paul's implied demythologisation of Gnostic and mystery ideas or John's complete elimination of apocalyptic eschatology, it is obvious the New Testament itself both permits and requires existential interpretation. It is precisely when its own mythological concepts are abandoned in favour of those of existential analysis that the dialectical character of the Christian life as freedom from the world and openness to it can be adequately represented.

---

[129] *Glauben und Verstehen*, I, p. 257; cf. also p. 167.

Bultmann insists that such a translation has a second important advantage. If life in faith is interpreted neither as an anxious apocalypticism nor as a new supernatural state, as an authentic understanding of one's existence as a person, then the modern man can understand the New Testament message. As soon as he sees that the content of this message is his own *existentiell* possibility, the "true σκάνδαλον" of the New Testament is no longer obscured by the pseudo scandal of its antiquated conceptuality.[130]

5. THE HISTORICITY OF MAN AND FAITH

We have seen now in some detail how Bultmann proposes to deal with the contemporary theological problem by undertaking an existential interpretation of the New Testament message. We have also seen that when such an interpretation is carried out, this message takes the form of "the Christian understanding of existence." In all of this, we have simply been trying to follow in an understanding way the steps in Bultmann's argument in "Neues Testament und Mythologie."

This line of approach must now be continued, for from this point forward, just as in all that has gone before, the logical structure and movement of Bultmann's thought correspond exactly with the development of his discussion in that essay. Given his understanding of the theological problem and the project he proposes as a solution to it, two questions inevitably arise that require to be answered. The purpose of the concluding half of the programmatic essay is to give answers to these questions, and our purpose here and in the section that follows must be to understand these answers. In pursuing this aim, we shall of course continue our practice of bringing to bear as

---

[130] Cf. *Kerygma und Mythos*, II, p. 188; also *Kerygma und Mythos*, III, pp. 50 f. (pp. 59 f.) and *Jesus Christ and Mythology*, pp. 36, 38 f.

much as possible the relevant materials from the larger corpus of Bultmann's writings.[131]

Having interpreted the New Testament message in terms of the understanding of existence it expresses, Bultmann must immediately face the question of the adequacy of his interpretation. This is made particularly necessary because, as he himself acknowledges, his existential interpretation has disregarded one thing the New Testament deems of utmost importance—that faith as the attitude of "authentic historicity" (*eigentliche Geschichtlichkeit*) is at the same time faith in Jesus Christ. "The New Testament affirms not only that faith, as the attitude of new and genuine life, is first present after a certain time—faith was 'revealed' and has 'come' (Gal. 3 : 23, 25)—for that could simply be a statement about cultural history (*Geistesgeschichte*), but that it has first become a *possibility* after a certain time, namely, as the result of an *occurrence*, the occurrence of Christ." Therefore, in the New Testament's view, "faith as an obedient surrender to God and inner freedom from the world is only possible as faith in Christ."[132]

The question, however, is whether an existential interpretation leads to a denial of this claim. "Is it a consequence of this kind of interpretation to eliminate the Christ-occurrence or to divest it of its scandalous character as an occurrence ?"[133]

Whatever answer is given to this question, at least some of the attempts to show that it must be answered affirmatively rest on misunderstandings of Bultmann's position. When Helmut Thielicke and others argue that "Bultmann's thinking . . . stands in the tradition of *Bewusstseinstheologie* (Schleiermacher, Ritschl, Herrmann)," or that what he means by a "self-understanding" is only verbally distinguishable from Lessing's timeless "truth of reason," they profoundly mis-

---

[131] In the case of the present section (as its title, indeed, is intended to suggest), the most important item is the essay "The Historicity of Man and Faith," *Existence and Faith*, pp. 92-110.

[132] *Kerygma und Mythos*, I, p. 31 (p. 22).   [133] *Ibid.*, p. 32 (p. 23).

represent his intention.[134]   If anything is certain about his theology, it is that it is informed by a very different ontology from that of the Enlightenment and the theologies that partook of the latter's spirit.   Therefore, while it may indeed fail to do justice to "the historical element in Christianity," the claim is quite unjustified that it has any *direct* parallels to traditional rationalism as represented, say, by a position like Lessing's.[135]

Bultmann himself has more than once pointed this out in his replies to his critics.[136] To be sure, he has allowed that his own unclear formulations may in part be to blame for the mis- understanding, and has suggested the reason for it may be a confusion between *existentiell* self-understanding and an existential or philosophical understanding of human existence. Since, as was pointed out in the preceding section, the second kind of understanding *is* theoretical in character, the proposi- tions to which it gives rise do indeed have the form of "time- less truths."   If, then, one fails to distinguish between it and an *existentiell* understanding, it is possible to assume that the latter also has a "timeless" or non-historical character. On the other hand, if one makes this distinction, the charge of "rationalism" seems completely unfounded.   In any case, there cannot be the slightest doubt that, for Bultmann, "the propositions of faith are not general truths."[137] He has con- sistently maintained the position expressed in an essay of 1931.

. . . *genuine faith in God* is to be sharply distinguished from what is customarily called a *world-view*. The knowledge of the power that creates and limits our existence is not a

---

[134] Cf. Helmut Thielicke, "Reflections on Bultmann's Hermeneutics," *Expository Times*, March, 1956, pp. 175 f. Cf. also *Kerygma und Mythos*, I, pp. 165 ff. (pp. 146 ff.). A criticism similar to Thielicke's has also been made by Walter Künneth in Ernst Kinder (ed.), *Ein Wort lutherischer Theologie zur Entmythologisierung*, Munich: Evangelischer Pressverband für Bayern, 1952, p. 78.

[135] Cf. Ian Henderson, *op. cit.*, pp. 39 ff.

[136] Cf. *Kerygma und Mythos*, II, pp. 201 f. (pp. 202 ff.); also *Jesus Christ and Mythology*, pp. 73 f.

[137] *Kerygma und Mythos*, II, p. 197 (p. 198).

theoretical knowledge, but, on the contrary, is a knowledge that breaks in upon us at critical moments in existence itself. It is never possessed as a secure possession or as a quieting insight, but rather constantly has to make its way against all the temptations that continually emerge out of existence and give man the illusion he can still dispose of himself and has his life in his own hands—even if it be by virtue of just such an insight. . . . Therefore, genuine faith in God is *not a general truth* which I acknowledge, of which I dispose, and which I apply. On the contrary, it is what it is only as something that constantly grows up and is laid hold of anew.[138]

If the charge of "rationalism" is unjustified, that of "mysticism" is equally so. Walter Künneth's statement, for example, that "Bultmann's dissolution of the category of the 'historically past, once-for-all, perfect,' in favour of the 'presently actual, calling to decision' moves in the sphere of mysticism's concept of religion"[139] receives no support whatever from Bultmann's writings. What he means by *existentiell* self-understanding has nothing to do with what is ordinarily and properly understood by mysticism. Indeed, the very term "self-understanding" suggests that what is meant is not some ineffable "feeling" or "ecstasy" involving a flight from history, but rather an "understanding" that takes place precisely *in* history with its encounters and claims.[140]

It may well be that Bultmann's interpretation is unable to express the claim that Christian faith is possible only as faith in Jesus Christ. But this can be responsibly shown only by respecting his clear intention and refraining from criticisms that really apply only to positions he himself has explicitly rejected.[141]

---

[138] *Glauben und Verstehen,* ii, pp. 6 f. (pp. 6 f.).

[139] Ernst Kinder (ed.), *op. cit.,* p. 78.

[140] Cf. especially *Glauben und Verstehen,* ii, pp. 8 f. (pp. 9 f.).

[141] Cf. the discussion of early liberal theology and the "history of religions school" in Sec. 3.

Having considered these typical misunderstandings, however, we must return to the question of adequacy. Characteristically, Bultmann himself does not permit this question to be silenced by simply pointing to the misunderstandings underlying certain of his critics' answers to it. On the contrary, with the almost ruthless honesty and self-consciousness that distinguish his entire work, he insists it also be raised about his own correctly understood existential interpretation. As a matter of fact, he even allows that this question has a particular relevance to the kind of interpretation he presents. For as soon as the New Testament is understood not as so much mythology, but as a summons to authentic existence, there are legitimate reasons for asking whether such an existence is possible only because of the occurrence of Christ. Bultmann is convinced this claim can continue to be made only when these reasons are considered. "The Christian faith can acquire self-confidence only when it has consistently thought through the possibility that it is impossible or unnecessary."[142]

But what are the reasons for questioning the New Testament's claim ? They have their basis, according to Bultmann, in the work of modern philosophy. If one takes seriously recent philosophical developments, it may well seem that the New Testament simply presents for the first time in cultural history (*Geistesgeschichte*) a significant expression of man's natural self-understanding. It may appear that what the kerygma expresses, in antiquated mythological concepts, is the same understanding of human life that contemporary philosophers have put forward under the phrase, "the historicity of man."[143] In the interesting correspondence of Graf Paul Yorck and Wilhelm Dilthey during the closing decade of the nineteenth century, there are already the nascent beginnings of such a "Christianity without Christ." Likewise, Karl Jaspers' more recent use of Kierkegaard's theology in developing a "philosophical faith" makes clear that it is possible to

[142] *Kerygma und Mythos*, I, p. 32 (p. 23). [143] Cf. *ibid.*

achieve an independent and non-mythological statement of the Christian self-understanding.[144]

Even more impressive is that "Martin Heidegger's existential analysis of *Dasein* seems to be simply a profane philosophical presentation of the New Testament view of human existence."[145] Bultmann points out that for Heidegger, just as for the New Testament, man is understood as a historical being who exists in care for himself on the basis of anxiety and is therefore constantly called to decide whether he will lose himself in the past, in the world of the "on hand" (*das Vorhandenen*) and the "one" (*das man*), or whether he will lay hold of his authentic existence by surrendering all his securities and unreservedly opening himself to the future. Bultmann notes significantly that when he is criticised for interpreting the New Testament in Heidegger's categories, he fears the real problem is overlooked. What should disturb his critics is that "philosophy all by itself already sees what the New Testament says."[146]

That Bultmann should speak in this way about Heidegger's philosophy may appear strange in the light of the understanding of philosophy briefly touched on in the preceding section. We saw there that, as Bultmann usually speaks of it, philosophy is understood to have a strictly formal function, in the sense of being an ontological analysis of the phenomenon of existence as such. Yet, as we also noted, many of his statements presuppose that philosophy has a material significance as well. Sometimes this tension in his view becomes quite explicit. In one place, for instance, he argues that theology would be made improperly dependent on philosophy "only if the concept of the authenticity of existence that philosophy develops implied a material ideal for existence, or, in other words, if philosophy prescribed to man, '*Thus* ought you to exist!' What philosophy tells him, however, is simply 'You ought to

[144] Cf. *ibid.*, pp. 32 f. (pp. 23 f.). [145] *Ibid.*, p. 33 (pp. 24 f.).
[146] *Ibid.* (p. 25).

exist !'—or, if that is already to say too much, it shows him what existence means."[147]   The uncertainty expressed in the last sentence, which, in effect, both affirms and denies philosophy a material as well as a formal import, illustrates the difficulty of Bultmann's view.

The most satisfactory explanation of this difficulty seems to be that Heidegger's fundamental concept of "existence," as briefly clarified in our earlier discussion, *is* a purely formal concept. To say that existence involves self-relatedness, that it is always uniquely mine, and that it takes place concretely only in the form of *some* specific self-understanding specifies no particular self-understanding and so says nothing whatever of a material or prescriptive nature. If, however, one further introduces the concepts of "authenticity" and "inauthenticity" of existence, a purely formal standpoint is abandoned. For though the concept of "authenticity," as Heidegger develops it, is not a "material ideal for existence" in the sense of prescribing some specific "what" of action, it does have a material import in the sense of specifying "how" an action must be performed if it is to be "authentic" rather than "inauthentic."[148] Therefore, at least *implicitly*, Heidegger's analysis of man in terms of the contrasting modes of authentic and inauthentic existence *does* prescribe a "material ideal for existence." Bultmann himself, indeed, seems to make this very point when he says in a recent essay that philosophical analysis is *indirectly* "genuine proclamation," that is, "a declaration that . . . addresses the hearer and summons him to a specific attitude."[149] But if this is so, the denial that philosophy prescribes any material ideal can only mean that it fails to specify any particular "what" of action, as distinguished from the mode or "how" in which all action ought to take place.

[147] *Kerygma und Mythos*, II, pp. 192 f. (p. 193).   Cf. also *Jesus Christ and Mythology*, pp. 55 f.

[148] Cf. Bultmann's own use of this distinction between "what" and "how" in *Existence and Faith*, p. 104; cf. also p. 203.

[149] *Glauben und Verstehen*, III, p. 122 (p. 236).

In any case, to suppose that Bultmann's denial means philosophy has no material import whatever makes it impossible to understand such statements as "philosophy all by itself already sees what the New Testament says." It may well be that the *direct* (or explicit) task of philosophy is not so much to summon man to an authentic existence as to make clear by phenomenological analysis what such existence means. Yet unless philosophy is also at least *indirectly* (or implicitly) a summons to authentic self-understanding, it can hardly threaten to take the place of the Christian kerygma. What bids fair to supplant theology is not philosophy in the sense of a formal ontological analysis, but a philosophy that, like Heidegger's, "calls man back to himself from his lostness in the 'one.' "[150]

A still more direct challenge to the Christian claim has been issued by one of Bultmann's former students. In a book originally published under the title, *Christentum und Selbstbehauptung*,[151] Wilhelm Kamlah has set forth on purely philosophical grounds "a secularised Christian understanding of existence." Bultmann holds that what Kamlah refers to as "self-giving" (*Hingabe*) and describes as an authentic self-understanding involving freedom from the past and openness for the future can be readily recognised as the same attitude the New Testament calls "faith." The sole but important difference is that, for Kamlah, actualisation of this attitude is not dependent on the event Jesus Christ. On the contrary, he argues that "philosophy as the true understanding of existence releases natural self-giving in all its truth" and so implies that revelation is unnecessary.[152]

From all of these philosophical developments, Bultmann draws the conclusion that there are legitimate reasons for

---

[150] *Kerygma und Mythos*, I, p. 35 (p. 27).

[151] Frankfurt: V. Klostermann, 1940. This volume has since been reissued in a second edition as *Christentum und Geschichtlichkeit*, Stuttgart: W. Kohlhammer Verlag, 1951.

[152] Cf. *Kerygma und Mythos*, I, p. 34 (pp. 25 f.).

questioning whether the New Testament's claim for the indispensability of the event of Christ can continue to be made. The theologian, he believes, must ask with all seriousness whether the attitude the New Testament refers to as "faith working through love" is simply man's natural self-understanding, which, given the legitimacy of the demand for an existential interpretation, may be more properly known and realised by philosophy than by theology.

Bultmann's own way of answering this question goes a considerable distance towards conceding philosophy's claim. It is quite correct, he holds, that faith "is not a mysterious, supernatural quality, but is the attitude of genuine humanity" and that love, likewise, "is not some mysterious, supernatural practice, but is man's 'natural' mode of relationship."[153] The New Testament itself makes this clear when it speaks of the believer as a "new creation," for such speaking obviously implies that the new existence realised "in Christ" is the very existence "natural" to man as God's creature.

Therefore, the claim of philosophy that the true nature of man can be discovered and known apart from the New Testament is not to be disputed. Although, from the standpoint of cultural history, philosophy has *not* discovered man's nature apart from the Christian tradition—what would existential philosophy be without the New Testament, without Luther, without Kierkegaard?—still this patent historical connection has nothing to do with the truth or falsity of philosophy's analysis of human existence. On the contrary, the very fact that the New Testament's concept of faith can be secularised and put forward as a possibility "natural" to man and discoverable through philosophical reflection "proves that Christian existence is nothing mysterious or supernatural."[154]

[153] *Ibid.* (p. 26). Cf. also *Existence and Faith*, pp. 107 f.

[154] *Kerygma und Mythos*, I, pp. 35 f. (pp. 26 f.). The doctrine that there is nothing "mysterious or supernatural" about the "content" (*das Was, das Gedankengehalt*) of the Christian faith and that it therefore is universally discoverable by man is one of the defining characteristics of Bultmann's theology.

The only question, then, that can be at issue between philosophy and theology is whether this Christian understanding of existence, which admittedly can be *known* apart from Christ, can also be *realised* apart from him. And here Bultmann believes the issue is sharply joined. For though philosophy and theology both agree that man as he actually is, is "fallen," they disagree quite radically about the precise character of this fallenness and therefore also about the conditions under which it can be overcome. According to philosophy, what is required in order to bring man to his authentic existence is that he be shown (or that he himself reflect on) what his true nature really is. In this sense, traditional idealism pronounces its *Werde, der du bist*! and Heidegger summons man to exist in freedom from his past and in openness to the future. Similarly, Kamlah places man under the demand of "self-giving" only because it is the imperative that arises from reflection on essential human nature.

From the New Testament's point of view, all this seems quite unjustified. "For it affirms that man cannot free himself from his actual fallenness in the world, but is freed by an act of God; and its proclamation is not a doctrine about man's 'nature,' his essential being, but is the proclamation of this very emancipating act, namely, the salvation-occurrence that has taken place in Christ."[155]   In other words, the New Testament asserts that without the saving act of God, the human situation is one of utter despair. For philosophy, on the other hand, man's situation neither is nor can be as desperate as theology is wont to portray it.

The reason for this difference is that although theology and philosophy both recognise that man can only become what in

---

Cf. especially *Existence and Faith*, pp. 61 ff., 96, 99 f.; *Glauben und Verstehen*, I, pp. 231, 236, 294-312; and *Glauben und Verstehen*, II, pp. 2, 49, 79-104, 272 (pp. 2, 55, 90-118, 302).

[155] *Kerygma und Mythos*, I, p. 35 (p. 27).

some sense he already is, they make very different judgments whether man as he actually exists already stands in his essential nature. Whereas philosophy holds that man's authentic existence is always open to him, the New Testament and theology affirm that this is not at all true of "the natural man," but solely of the believer who has already permitted himself to be freed by God's emancipating act. In short, philosophy looks upon fallenness as something man himself can escape once he has clearly grasped his situation, and therefore regards it as a condition that does not extend to his inmost self. By contrast, the New Testament "affirms that man himself is completely and utterly fallen."[156]

But does this affirmation not deny what is clearly attested by philosophy, that man can know about his fallenness ? Not at all, Bultmann replies. It is precisely the man who is actually fallen who can know that he is not who he essentially is and ought to be. Indeed, such knowledge of one's authentic existence belongs to every human life, for "one would not exist as a man, even as a fallen man, if he did not know about and was not concerned about what he truly is."[157] Nevertheless, what is to be disputed in philosophy's claim is that knowledge of one's authenticity already gives one the power to realise it. Although philosophy recognises that man does not always in fact realise his authentic existence, it still assumes that this existence is at all times capable of realisation. "You can," it says, "because you ought !" Consequently, "it already takes for a possibility in fact what is really only a possibility in principle. In the New Testament's judgment, however, man has lost the factual possibility and, indeed, even his knowledge of his authenticity is falsified by being bound up with the assumption that he has power over it."[158]

Therefore, the position of theology *vis-à-vis* the claim of

[156] *Ibid.*, p. 36 (p. 29).
[157] *Ibid.*; cf. also *Glauben und Verstehen*, ii, p. 120 (p. 136).
[158] *Kerygma und Mythos*, i, p. 37 (p. 29).

modern philosophy has to be the same as that of the New Testament in face of the analogous claims of Jewish legalism and the Gnostics' striving for "wisdom." Such claims express man's ancient assumption that his true being lies within his own power, so that he himself can realise his authentic existence. Philosophy fails to recognise that in the condition of fallenness, *every* act of man, including most especially the attempt to escape from it, is a fallen act. Therefore, just as, according to Paul, the Jew who was zealous for "righteousness" missed the very thing he sought because the same fundamental attitude of self-glorification and "wilfulness" (*Eigenmächtigkeit*) still governed his "works," so also the modern man who tries to be "self-giving" finally succeeds only "in drawing even self-giving within the sphere of his wilfulness and thus ends in self-contradiction."[159] That this happens in the case of Heidegger, Bultmann believes, is quite evident even though Heidegger does not characterise the attitude of "resolution" (*Entschlossenheit*) as "self-giving," for "the taking over of one's 'thrownness' [*Geworfenheit*] in resolution in face of death is an act of radical wilfulness."[160] Likewise, the "self-giving" to which Kamlah summons man is itself a wilful act, and so he never succeeds in showing that man has any other possibility apart from Christ than to despair of his existence.

In any event, the New Testament addresses man as one who is wilful through and through and holds that, although he can very well know he does not have an authentic life, he still is powerless to lay hold of his life because he is completely fallen under the bondage of sin. Sin, according to the New Testament, is just this attitude of wilfulness and self-glorification in which man tries to realise his own existence.

This implies that the concept of sin is something more than a mythical concept. To claim that the statement that man is a sinner is simply an unnecessary mythological interpretation of an ontological truth would be legitimate only if the natural

[159] *Ibid.* (p. 30).   [160] *Ibid.*; also *Existence and Faith*, pp. 107 f.

man as such could recognise his wilfulness as guilt. For him to be able to do this would in turn depend on whether or how radically he could understand his existence completely as a gift. "But it is just this possibility against which he has closed himself in his radical wilfulness ; he looks upon his existence as a task he himself must lay hold of and master."[161] In other words, man is blind to the full extent of his fallenness and must accordingly look upon theology's talk of "sin" as so much unnecessary mythology. That such talk is *not* mythology, however, becomes clear to him in the moment in which he is encountered by the love of God as the power that embraces and bears with him even in this final expression of his radical fallenness.[162]

If man as a whole is fallen in his wilfulness and, in spite of a knowledge of his authenticity, is unable to realise it, his true life becomes a possibility *in fact* for him only when he is freed from himself. But just this is what is proclaimed by the New Testament when it speaks of the occurrence of Christ. It announces that God acts and has acted where man himself is completely powerless.

That this is the meaning of the Christ-occurrence as the New Testament speaks of it, Bultmann holds to be unmistakable. Whether one considers the formulations of Paul or those of John, the heart of their proclamation is that Christ is the revelation of the love of God, which frees man from himself and for himself by freeing him for a life of self-giving in faith and love (cf. II Cor. 5 : 17-21 ; John 5 : 24 ff.). In this, the New Testament simply assumes that faith is possible only as faith in God's love. But then it goes on to claim that "faith in the love of God is actually wilfulness as long as such love is mere wishful thinking or an idea, as long as God him-

---

[161] *Kerygma und Mythos*, I, p. 38 (p. 31).

[162] Bultmann's point here should be carefully noted, for contrary to certain interpreters (e.g. Ian Henderson, *op. cit.*, pp. 17 f.), he does *not* hold that sin is a "mythological concept" that sets a limit to demythologisation. Cf. also *Kerygma und Mythos*, I, pp. 123 f. (pp. 104 f.).

self has not revealed it. Hence the reason Christian faith is faith in Christ is because it is faith in the revealed love of God."[163] The New Testament holds that we are free to give ourselves to God and our neighbour only because God has already given himself for us in Jesus Christ (cf. I John 4 : 10, 19).

Bultmann concludes that "what decisively distinguishes the New Testament from philosophy and the Christian faith from 'natural' self-understanding is that the New Testament speaks about and Christian faith knows about *an act of God that first makes possible man's self-giving, his faith, his love—in short, his authentic life*."[164] Accordingly, the answer that must be given to the question of whether the New Testament means by "faith" nothing but what philosophy speaks of as "the historicity of man" is both yes and no.[165] For although in its existential meaning, faith is nothing other than man's original possibility of authentic existence, which philosophy also properly knows and proclaims, theology must deny that man as such can realise this possibility and affirm instead that it becomes a possibility in fact for him only in consequence of God's saving act in Jesus Christ.

6. THE DEMYTHOLOGISATION OF THE CHRIST-OCCURRENCE

The question that arises now is whether this affirmation sets a limit to the demythologisation of the New Testament message. According to Bultmann, "what the New Testament says in mythological language about the existence of man prior to faith may be demythologised, as may be also what it says about the existence of the believer. But the question remains whether the affirmation that the transition from the

---

[163] *Kerygma und Mythos*, I, p. 39 (p. 32).   [164] *Ibid.*, p. 40 (p. 33).
[165] Cf. *ibid.*, p. 34 (p. 26).

former existence to the latter . . . is conceivable only as an act of God, and that faith can be actual only as faith in the love of God revealed in Christ—whether this affirmation is a mythological affirmation."[166]

Bultmann makes clear that this question means, first of all, whether the event of Christ is a mythical event. He holds that the larger issue of whether *any* speaking about an act of God must be mythological need not be dealt with until this first question has been answered. Accordingly, the problem to which he next turns and in the discussion of which we must attempt to follow him is whether the event of Christ as the saving act of God is a mythical event.

Bultmann begins by granting that the New Testament undoubtedly presents the Christ-occurrence as a mythical occurrence. But the question, he thinks, is whether it must be so interpreted or whether "the New Testament itself already puts us on the way towards a demythologising interpretation."[167] He believes the latter is actually the case and if the Christ-event is understood from the standpoint of the New Testament's "true intention" in speaking of it, it will be seen not to be a mythical event at all. Indeed, he is so clear about this that it is difficult to comprehend why several of his interpreters have misunderstood his position. To argue, as Henderson does, that "here is the point where Bultmann calls a halt to the process of demythologising,"[168] or, as Macquarrie does, that "Bultmann himself seems to concede that we can speak of God's acts only in mythical terms"[169] is

[166] *Ibid.*, p. 40 (p. 33). The second sentence as given here is based on an emendation approved by Prof. Bultmann himself in a letter of July 23, 1956. "I must be grateful," he wrote, "for your letter of the 15th, for it brought to my attention that I have been guilty of an oversight in the formulation of an important sentence. In the short form [*sic* of the sentence as it presently stands in the printed text] I intended to say what you have expressed in the longer form; but my short form is wrong, and I am amazed that neither I myself nor my other readers have previously noticed it. I rejoice all the more, therefore, that you have caught the error. The sentence must read as you have written," whereupon follows the corrected formulation given above.

[167] *Ibid.*, pp. 40 f. (p. 34).   [168] *Op. cit.*, p. 17.   [169] *Op. cit.*, p. 174.

completely to miss Bultmann's evident intention. The whole point of the concluding section of the programmatic essay, as well as of many earlier statements,[170] is to show that the Christ-occurrence is *not* a mythical occurrence (in the strict sense in which Bultmann himself uses the term "myth") and therefore there need be no limit to demythologising the New Testament message. Bultmann's success in showing this may be questioned. But there is no doubt whatever that this is what he intends to do.

His first step in realising his intention is simply to note that the Christ-occurrence is not mythical in the same sense as the Greek or Hellenistic deities are, since its central elements are the person and destiny of the actual historical figure Jesus of Nazareth. This alone, he holds, already raises the question of whether it is really a mythical occurrence at all. But even more important is that the details of the myths in which the figure of Christ is presented are mutually contradictory, as is quite obviously the case, with the myth of pre-existence and the legend of the virgin birth or with the interpretation of the resurrection as exaltation and the conflicting legends of the empty tomb and the ascension. Such contradictions leave no doubt that the "true intention" of the christological myths cannot be discerned in the meaning of their objective contents, but must be uncovered through critical interpretation.[171]

These two considerations together prompt the question whether the real purpose of the mythological concepts in which the New Testament explicates its christology is not simply to express the existential "significance" (*Bedeutsamkeit*) of the historical figure of Jesus as the salvation-occurrence. This clearly seems to be so of the statements concerning pre-existence and virgin birth ; for what they evidently intend to say when they present Jesus as having come from heaven or

[170] Cf., e.g., *Existence and Faith*, pp. 75-79, 197 ff., 301, n. 7.
[171] Cf. *Kerygma und Mythos*, I, p. 41 (pp. 34 f.); also *Glauben und Verstehen*, I, pp. 245-267, especially pp. 262-267.

as having had a non-natural origin is that his "significance" for faith is not exhausted by ordinary historical observation. The "actual meaning" (*wirkliche Bedeutung*) of his person and destiny is not to be discerned in their objective historical givenness, but solely in the possibility they present to me for understanding *existentiell* the meaning of my existence—or, as Bultmann puts it, "in what God wills to say to me through [them]."[172]

A similar judgment may also be made about the New Testament's other christological statements. Bultmann holds it is just when these statements are interpreted not in terms of their objective contents, but as statements of existential significance that their "true intention" is rightly grasped. The decisive proof of this, he believes, is the way the New Testament presents the central events of Jesus' crucifixion and resurrection.

Bultmann concedes, of course, that if we simply follow the New Testament's objective statements, the cross is undoubtedly understood as a mythical event. What such statements generally present is the crucifixion of the pre-existent and sinless Son of God, whose death as a man is either a propitiatory or a substitutionary sacrifice that frees mankind from the punishment of death by atoning for its guilt (cf. Rom. 3 : 25 f. ; Gal. 3 : 13 ; II Cor. 5 : 21). Yet even within the New Testament, it becomes clear that such an interpretation, which derives its concepts from the cultic and juristic thinking of Judaism, does not adequately convey what faith intends to say. Faith's claim is not simply that Christ's death frees man from the guilt and punishment of sin, but that the believer in the cross is also freed from sin's *power* (cf. Col. 2: 13-15).[173] Thus Paul, for example, finally has recourse to the concepts of the mystery religions and Gnosticism because they enable him to express more adequately than Jewish concepts the full

---

[172] *Kerygma und Mythos*, I, p. 41 (p. 35).
[173] Cf. *ibid.*, pp. 39, 42 (pp. 32, 36).

significance of the crucifixion. By presenting the cross as the death of a mystery deity in which the believer may participate through baptism and sacramental communion, or as a cosmic event in which the powers of "this world" are decisively defeated, the conviction is more appropriately conveyed that the power as well as the guilt of sin has been overcome.[174]

But even these Hellenistic mythologies are finally broken by the critical way in which the New Testament authors make use of them. As we have already seen from our discussion of Paul's doctrine of the sacraments in Section 4, the New Testament rejects the mystery religions' notion that the salvation present in the death of the divinity may be realised in the believer apart from his own freedom and responsibility. It insists, rather, that the cross of Christ, *as the salvation-event*, is "a genuinely historical event" (*ein echt geschichtliches Ereignis*) that takes place either as salvation or as judgment precisely *in* the individual's decision of faith or unfaith. Likewise, Gnostic concepts also are decisively qualified. Whereas for Gnosticism, the salvation-event is literally understood as a cosmic occurrence that has taken place in the mythical past, for the New Testament, it is a historical event that always occurs only in the present. This is evident, on the one hand, from the *existentiell* rather than "objective" character of the "word" or "tradition" through which the Christ-event is made known and, on the other hand, from the interpretation of "faith" in this word as something different from objective knowledge, either of facts or of principles.[175] "To believe in the cross," Bultmann writes, "does not mean to look at some mythical process that has taken place outside of us and our world, or at an event that is objectively visible and that God has somehow reckoned to our credit. Rather, it means to

[174] Cf. *Theologie des Neuen Testaments*, pp. 297 ff. (I, pp. 298 ff.).

[175] Cf. especially Bultmann's discussion of "the concept of revelation in the New Testament," *Existence and Faith*, pp. 71-91; also *Glauben und Verstehen*, I, pp. 180 f., 208 f.

accept the cross as one's own and to allow oneself to be crucified with Christ."[176]

Accordingly, while for the New Testament Christ's crucifixion is not an isolated event that happens to some mystery deity, but rather is an event that has genuinely "cosmic" dimensions, this must be understood very differently from the apparently similar view of Gnosticism. What happens in the cross is not some quasi-natural process by which man's innermost being is set free from its fateful subjection to "matter," but rather the presentation of a possibility for understanding one's existence that is relevant to all men everywhere and can be actualised by them whenever they appropriate it through their individual decisions.[177] Thus the New Testament speaks of the cross as "the eschatological event," which never becomes an event of the past, but rather is constantly present both in preaching and sacraments (cf. II Cor. 6 : 2 ; Rom. 6 : 3, 6 ; I Cor. 11 : 26) and the believer's way of conducting his life (II Cor. 4 : 10 f. ; Gal. 5 : 24 ; 6 : 14 ; Phil. 3 : 10).[178]

In sum, "the cross of Christ as the salvation-occurrence is not a mythical event at all, but rather a historical occurrence [*ein geschichtliches Geschehen*] that has its origin in the event [*das historische Ereignis*] of the crucifixion of Jesus of Nazareth."[179] In its "historical significance" (*geschichtliche Bedeutsamkeit*), or in the *existentiell* possibility it presents for under-

---

[176] *Kerygma und Mythos*, I, p. 42 (p. 36).

[177] Cf. *Theologie des Neuen Testaments*, pp. 302 f. (I, pp. 302 f.); also *Das Urchristentum*, pp. 218-233 (pp. 196-208).

[178] Cf. *Kerygma und Mythos*, I, pp. 42 f. (pp. 36 f.).

[179] *Ibid.*, p. 43 (p. 37). The distinction here between *historisch* and *geschichtlich*, which Bultmann frequently (though by no means always) employs to express two different senses of the word "historical," first became current in modern theology as a result of the book of Martin Kähler, *Der sogenannte historische Jesus und der geschichtliche, biblische Christus* (new edition by Ernst Wolf, Munich: Christian Kaiser Verlag, 1953). Bultmann's own use of the distinction is probably best clarified in the light of his basic philosophical presuppositions. In terms of our earlier discussion in Sec. 4, we may say it expresses the fundamental contrast between "objective" and "*existentiell*" (or "is" and "ought") as applied either to the reality of history or to the understanding of it.

standing one's existence, Jesus' death is the judgment of the "world" that frees all who appropriate it for authentic historical existence.

In this sense, and not in the sense of some theory of satisfaction or sacrifice, Christ is crucified "for us." Bultmann concludes: "It is precisely *not* to mythological, but to historical [*geschichtlich*] understanding that the event of the cross [*das historische Ereignis des Kreuzes*] discloses itself as the salvation-event ; for it is the nature of genuine historical understanding to understand an event in its significance. What the mythological language finally wants to do is nothing other than to express the significance of the event of the cross. In the significance that belongs to it, this event has created a new historical situation ; and the proclamation of the cross asks its hearer whether he will appropriate this meaning, whether he is willing to be crucified with Christ."[180]

The question now is how this meaning is to be seen. Does the significance of the cross depend on its being the cross of *Christ* ? Must one first become convinced of Christ's significance before he can discern the meaning of the cross ? And does this imply, finally, that one must understand the cross as the cross of the historical Jesus in order to understand its existential significance ?

Bultmann's answer to these questions, both in the programmatic essay and in his other writings, has been quite generally misunderstood, especially by his English-speaking critics. It is widely held that he denies all real continuity between the Jesus of history and the crucified Christ of the kerygma, and in fact presents the former, in Macquarrie's phrase, as "simply a teacher of practical philosophy."[181] This view, with certain

---

[180] *Kerygma und Mythos*, I, p. 43 (p. 37).

[181] *Op. cit.*, p. 80; cf. also pp. 23 and 179. Similar views are expressed by Henderson, *op. cit.*, p. 49; Miegge, *op. cit.*, pp. 26 f. and 125-137; and Geraint Vaughan Jones, *Christology and Myth in the New Testament*, New York: Harper & Brothers, 1956, pp. 122 and 163. Cf. the brief discussion in *Existence and Faith*, pp. 11 f.

qualifications, has recently been given further currency by the monograph of James M. Robinson, *A New Quest of the Historical Jesus.*[182] According to Robinson, "the classical Bultmannian position" involves the "repudiation" of a quest of the historical Jesus as both "impossible" and "illegitimate."[183] Robinson allows that there is an "undercurrent" in Bultmann's earlier writings that moves in a contrary direction from the "classical" position ; and he further argues that, under growing pressures from certain of his leading students, Bultmann has "shifted" his more recent position in the direction of the underlying tendency in his early work.[184] Even so, Robinson's main point is that a new quest of the historical Jesus involves "a critical revision of Bultmann's position," and so is in the strict sense "post-Bultmannian." Until the quite recent "shift" in Bultmann's thinking, the dominant emphasis in his writings has been on the impossibility and illegitimacy of a concern with the Jesus of history.

If this view is correct, one would naturally expect Bultmann simply to deny that there is any need whatever to understand the historical Jesus in order to understand his cross in its existential significance. In fact, however, he does not do this at all. On the contrary, he affirms quite clearly that there must indeed have been such a prior understanding in the case of the first disciples. "They experienced the cross of him with whom they were bound in the living present. And it was out of this personal bond, in which the cross was an event in their own lives, that it became a question for them and revealed to them its meaning."[185] Elsewhere, Bultmann has spoken to the same point even more conclusively. "The decision that Jesus' disciples had once made to accept his having been sent from God by 'following' him had to be made anew and radically in consequence of his crucifixion. *The cross*, so to say, raised once again the question of decision; for little as it

---

[182] London: S.C.M. Press, Ltd., 1959. [183] *Ibid.*, p. 12.
[184] *Ibid.*, p. 19; also n. 1. [185] *Kerygma und Mythos*, I, p. 43 (p. 38).

could call in question the 'what' [*das Was*] of Jesus' proclamation, all the more it could and did make questionable the 'that' [*das Dass*]—his legitimation, his assertion that it was God's messenger bringing the final decisive word."[186]   For the first believers, the meaning of the cross was most profoundly dependent on the significance of Jesus' total life and work as they had experienced them.   Indeed, when Bultmann says the cross raised "once again" the *same* question of decision that Jesus himself had raised in his proclamation and the *same* decision that had been made already in Jesus' lifetime to "follow" him had to be "made anew" as a result of the crucifixion, he affirms a strict and unbroken continuity between the Jesus of history and the crucified redeemer.

The thing to note, however, is that, so far from simply being an "undercurrent" or a "shift" in Bultmann's thought, the affirmation of such continuity has been the exclusive tendency of his position for over three decades.   He has repeatedly made clear in his several accounts of the development of New Testament christology that this development can be made historically intelligible only if one recognises the fundamental continuity between the message of the historical Jesus and the church's proclamation of the crucified Lord.[187]

On the other hand, Bultmann has also recognised that our position to-day is very different from that of the original disciples.   "For us," he writes, "this personal bond [*sic* with the historical Jesus] cannot be reproduced, and it is not out of it that the meaning of the cross can disclose itself to us. As an event of the past the cross is no longer an event in our own lives ; we know of it as a historical event [*ein historisches Ereignis*] only by historical report."[188]   Bultmann's point, it will be noted, is not that we to-day cannot know the cross as a

---

[186] *Theologie des Neuen Testaments*, p. 47 (i, pp. 44 f.).

[187] Cf. especially *Glauben und Verstehen*, i, pp. 204 f., 265 f.; and *Theologie des Neuen Testaments*, pp. 45-56 (i, pp. 42-53).   Cf. also *Existence and Faith*, pp. 194 ff.

[188] *Kerygma und Mythos*, i, pp. 43 f. (p. 38).

historical event or that a contemporary historian cannot understand the significance of the cross in the light of Jesus' total ministry. Rather, what he denies is that anyone now can so understand the meaning of the cross *in the same direct and unmediated way in which it was grasped by the first disciples*—namely, as an event in their own lives set in the context of their personal experience of Jesus' life and work. If we to-day are to understand the meaning of the cross by first understanding it as the cross of the historical Jesus, this can only be done—but it actually *can* done!—by the indirect and laborious process of historical reconstruction.[189]

Bultmann holds, however, that while such a process is possible, it is hardly necessary. For "the crucified one is not at all proclaimed in the New Testament in such a way that the meaning of the cross would be disclosed from his historical life as reproduced by historical research. On the contrary, he is proclaimed as the crucified one who is at the same time the risen Lord. The cross and the resurrection belong together as a unity."[190]

But what is to be made of the resurrection? Is it not a mythical event *sensu strictissimo*?

Bultmann readily grants that the resurrection is not a historical event (*ein historisches Ereignis*) which, like the crucifixion, is to be understood in its existential significance. What does seem to him to be so is that the New Testament's statements about the resurrection are its attempt to express the decisive meaning of the cross for human existence. They intend to say simply that Jesus' crucifixion is not to be viewed merely as a human death, but is to be seen as God's redemptive judgment of the world, which frees man from himself, and so deprives death of its power.[191]

[189] Bultmann himself has provided such a reconstruction in his book, *Jesus*, Tübingen: J. C. B. Mohr, 3rd ed., 1951 (English translation by L. P. Smith and E. H. Lantero in Rudolf Bultmann, *Jesus and the Word*, New York: Charles Scribner's Sons, 2nd ed., 1958).

[190] *Kerygma und Mythos*, I, p. 44 (p. 38).   [191] Cf. *ibid.*

The evidence for this, Bultmann believes, is that the New Testament presents the cross and the resurrection as a single event, which as such is the "cosmic" occurrence through which mankind is judged and the possibility of new life created for all who will appropriate it in faith (cf. Rom. 4 : 25). This implies, he claims, that the resurrection cannot be adequately understood as a second historical event alongside the event of the cross. The New Testament itself seems to recognise this when it makes clear (as, for instance, in the *double entendre* of John's phrase "to be lifted up") that the one who is crucified is already the Son of God and that even in the occurrence of his death the power of death has already been overcome.[192]

Still, Bultmann admits there are places in the New Testament—for example, the legends of the empty tomb and the Easter stories that report Jesus' *post-mortem* appearances (cf. Luke 24 : 39-43)—where the resurrection is clearly presented as a second historical event. He also allows that there is little point in arguing that these synoptic legends and stories are relatively late constructions which were almost certainly unknown to the earliest church. For in at least one place, even the Apostle Paul undertakes to prove the resurrection's objective historicity. Karl Barth notwithstanding, Paul's enumeration of the eye-witnesses in 1 Corinthians 15 : 3-8 can be nothing other than "an attempt to make the resurrection of Christ credible as an objective historical fact."[193]

Nevertheless, Barth's forced exegesis indirectly suggests that what the New Testament itself really wants to affirm when it speaks of Jesus' being raised from the dead cannot be affirmed if his resurrection is simply a miraculous historical event. As faith understands it, Christ's resurrection involves far more than the resuscitation of an isolated human corpse ; for it is "the eschatological event" in which the power of death in general, or for *all* men, has finally been overcome (cf.

[192] Cf. *ibid.* (p. 39).
[193] *Glauben und Verstehen*, 1, p. 54. Cf. *Kerygma und Mythos*, 1, pp. 44 f. (p. 39).

II Tim. 1 : 10).[194] This is why Paul presses into service the concepts of the Gnostic myth of redemption. He wants to convey the faith that just as in Christ's death *all* have died (II Cor. 5 : 14 f.), so also in his resurrection " will *all* be made alive" (I Cor. 15 : 22). In fact, Paul even speaks of the risen life with Christ as already realised in the present, namely, through baptism (cf Rom. 6 : 4 f. ; 6 : 11) and in the believers' manner of living "as men who have been brought from death to life" (Rom. 6 : 13 ; cf. I Thess. 5 : 5-8).[195]

Here, too, however, the Gnostic mythology is radically qualified by the New Testament writers. The very fact that in Romans 6 : 13 participation in Christ's resurrection is a matter of imperative demand as well as an indicative state makes clear that it is understood quite differently than a consistent Gnosticism would understand it. So far from being a pre-existent "nature" once for all set free by the "redeemed redeemer's" exaltation, the resurrected life in Christ is an *existentiell* possibility that must continually be realised anew through the responsible decisions of the individual believer.[196]

Thus Bultmann affirms that *"faith in the resurrection is nothing other than faith in the cross as the salvation-event*, or, as may also be said, as the cross of Christ."[197] It is not, he holds, as though there were two objects of faith, so that one could first be led to believe in Christ by being persuaded of his miraculous resurrection and, then, on that basis also come to believe in his cross. On the contrary, to believe in Christ is nothing other than to believe in the cross as God's act of salvation. "The cross is not the salvation-event because it is the cross of Christ ; it is the cross of Christ because it is the salvation-event. Apart from this it is merely the tragic end of a noble man."[198]

But if this is so, our earlier question, how the significance

---

[194] Cf. *Kerygma und Mythos*, I, p. 45 (p. 40).
[195] Cf. *ibid.*, pp. 45 f. (pp. 40 f.).
[196] Cf. *Das Urchristentum*, pp. 225 f. (p. 202).
[197] *Kerygma und Mythos*, I, p. 46 (p. 41).   [198] *Ibid.*

of the cross as the act of God is to be discerned, is still unanswered. If the resurrection is not an event that objectively proves the significance of the cross, but rather is itself precisely identical with this significance, how is it that we come to believe in the cross as the salvation-event ?

Bultmann believes there is only one answer to be given to this question: We come to believe in the cross as the event of salvation because it is proclaimed as such, because the crucified Jesus is proclaimed as the risen Lord. But this means, he argues, that it is illegitimate to attempt to get behind this proclamation in order to justify it on the basis of its historical origins. His point, it should be noted, is not that the proclamation may not be made historically intelligible by tracing its continuity with the message of the historical Jesus. Rather, what he rejects is the effort to *prove* the proclamation by adducing objective historical grounds for believing it. By its very nature as an *existentiell* summons, the message of the resurrection is something concerning whose truth we neither can nor may inquire by objective historical means, but which, rather, asks us ourselves whether we are willing to believe it.

On the other hand, this does not mean that faith is an arbitrary decision to believe something unintelligible simply at the bidding of an external authority. On the contrary, "in commanding us to believe in the death and resurrection of Christ as the eschatological occurrence, [the proclamation] puts its question to us in such a way that it thereby opens up the possibility of an understanding of ourselves."[199] This it can do because "the possibility of [its] being understood coincides with the possibility of man's understanding himself. What he is asked is whether he is *willing* to understand himself as the word instructs him. In the fact that he *can* thus understand himself lies the sole criterion of the word's truth— or better expressed, perhaps, it is to this alone that the man

[199] *Ibid.*

who asks for a criterion is referred."[200] Accordingly, Bultmann concludes that faith and unfaith are not matters of "a blind and arbitrary resolve," but are "an understanding yes or no" in response to the word of proclamation.[201]

But does this answer also hold good of the original believers ? Did they, too, only come to believe in the significance of the cross or in the reality of the resurrection because they were asked to believe in it by the proclamation ? For them, at least, was not the course of events exactly reversed, was it not because of the event of the resurrection that the proclamation itself came into existence ?

Bultmann's answer is both yes and no. Although, as we have seen, he denies that the resurrection either was or could have been an objective historical event, he has never denied that the resurrection is a reality independent of faith or that the emergence of the Easter faith among the original community was in some sense subsequent to the reality of the resurrection itself. To be sure, the truth of this statement has frequently been challenged by Bultmann's more conservative critics, who have agreed with the claims of Karl Barth that for Bultmann "the real Easter-event . . . is the rise of the Easter faith of the first disciples" and "the 'act of God' " in which their faith was based "was identical with the fact they believed."[202] In fact, however, Bultmann expresses his view with great caution in order to avoid precisely this kind of misunderstanding : "The Easter-event, *insofar as it can be spoken of as an objective event* [*ein historisches Ereignis*] alongside of the cross, is nothing other than the rise of faith in the risen one in which the proclamation had its origin. The Easter-event *as the resurrection of Christ* is not an objective event [*kein historisches Ereignis*] . . . [but, as Bultmann expresses it

---

[200] *Glauben und Verstehen*, i, p. 284; cf. *Kerygma und Mythos*, iii, pp. 57 f. (pp. 69 f.).

[201] *Kerygma und Mythos*, i., p. 46 (pp. 41 f.). Cf. *Existence and Faith*, pp. 55 f.

[202] *Kerygma und Mythos*, ii, pp. 104 f.

on the preceding page,] the eschatological fact of the annihilation of the power of death in general."[203]

Bultman clearly distinguishes between (1) *the reality of the resurrection itself*, which, while not an objective event at all, still is independently real as the gracious action of God whereby we are presented with the factual possibility of authentic existence, and (2) *the first occurrence of faith in the resurrection*, which *is* an objective event open to the historian's scrutiny. Thus he can allow for the affirmation by faith of the independent reality of the resurrection as the ground of the Easter message and also maintain that what the historian can see is simply that this message in fact arose within the circle of Jesus' disciples and that the occasion (or occasions) for its arising probably took the form of some kind of visionary experience in which Jesus was apprehended as the exalted Messiah.[204]

In this sense, Bultmann can readily agree that for the original believers the reality of the resurrection itself preceded the emergence of the Easter faith and proclamation. For though the precedence here was not that of one objective historical event to another, there can be no question that the initial appearance of the Christian faith and kerygma was of the nature of a response—and a response, moreover, to a divine reality outside of them and prior to them.[205]

On the other hand, Bultmann also makes clear that, even for the first community, the faith and message of Easter were in another sense a response to a human word of proclamation. We saw earlier that, contrary to a prevalent misunderstanding, Bultmann emphasises the continuity between the message of the Jesus of history and the church's proclamation of the

---

[203] *Kerygma und Mythos*, I, pp. 46, 45 (pp. 42, 40); italics added.

[204] Cf. *ibid.*, pp. 46 f. (p. 42); and p. 171 (p. 152), where Thielicke quotes a statement of Bultmann's to this effect. Cf. also Bultmann's review of Emmanuel Hirsch, *Die Auferstehungsgeschichten und der christliche Glaube*, in *Theologische Literaturzeitung*, September-October, 1940, pp. 242-246.

[205] Cf. *Kerygma und Mythos*, II, pp. 204 ff. (pp. 206-209).

crucified Lord. But an implication of such continuity is that *the church's faith in the resurrection was in reality its way of responding to the ministry of the historical Jesus.* Thus the passage cited on page 96 to show that the event of the cross raised once again the same question of decision Jesus had already raised by his preaching continues with the sentence: "The church had to overcome the scandal of the cross and did so with the Easter faith."[206] In another place, Bultmann makes the same point by saying that the historical Jesus' call for decision with reference to his person as bearer of the word "implies a christology . . . that makes explicit the answer to his question and so expresses the obedience that acknowledges in him God's revelation. Such a christology became explicit in the primitive community to the extent that they understood Jesus as the one whom God has made Messiah by the resurrection."[207]

In short, the life and proclamation of the historical Jesus were the objective historical occasion for the Easter faith and message of the first disciples. And in this sense even theirs was a faith for which a human proclamation was a prior and determining factor.

But this means that for the first believers, just as for those of every succeeding generation, Jesus' saving significance was visible only to the eyes of faith, or, in other words, was a matter of *existentiell* decision in face of a more or less explicit summons to believe. Therefore, so far from being an objective historical testimony that can be detached from the reality it attests, the Easter faith and proclamation of the first community are themselves constituent elements in the event of salvation. "The word of proclamation that had its origin in the Easter-event belongs to the eschatological salvation-occurrence."[208] Paul clearly indicates this, Bultmann believes, when he affirms that "God's act of salvation consists in his

---

[206] *Theologie des Neuen Testaments*, p. 47 (1, p. 45).
[207] *Ibid.*, p 46 (1, pp. 43 f.).   [208] *Kerygma und Mythos*, 1, p. 47 (p. 42).

having instituted the *'ministry* of reconciliation' or the *'word* of reconciliation' (II Cor. 5 : 18 f.) and that the *gospel* is the 'power of God for salvation to everyone who has faith' (Rom. 1 : 16."[209] It is precisely the "word" that, as Luther put it, is "added to" the cross and makes it understandable as the salvation-occurrence by asking man whether he will understand himself as one who has been crucified with Christ and so also raised with him to new life. In the moment in which the word sounds forth through preaching or sacraments, the cross and resurrection are concretely represented as an *existentiell* possibility, and the eschatological day of judgment and salvation is actually realised (cf. II Cor. 6 : 2). *"Christ crucified and risen encounters us in the word of proclamation and nowhere else. And faith in this word is the true faith of Easter.* . . . It is the faith that the word proclaimed is the authorised word of God."[210]

But this implies that, just as the faith of the believer and the word of proclamation belong to the salvation-occurrence, so also does the church as the community in and through which the word continues to be proclaimed and within which individual believers are gathered as those who have already passed into eschatological existence. According to Bultmann, "the word of God and the church belong together, insofar as it is through the word that the church is constituted as the community of those who have been called and insofar as the proclamation of the word is not the statement of a general truth, but an authorised proclamation that as such has need of a legitimated bearer."[211] In its momentary confession of faith, whether through preaching or sacraments, the church gives to the word of God its indispensable character as event and so provides the actual locus for the continued occurrence of the event of salvation. But this means the church itself is

---

[209] *Existence and Faith*, p. 77.   [210] *Kerygma und Mythos*, I, p. 46 (pp. 41 f.).
[211] *Kerygma und Mythos*, II, p. 206 (p. 209). Cf. also *Glauben und Verstehen*, I, pp. 180 f.

real only as an event. In its true nature, it is not an objective (*historisches*) phenomenon, but rather a historical (*geschichtliches*) phenomenon that is only paradoxically identical with any sociological structure or institutional form.[212]

This, then, is the evidence that seems to Bultmann to warrant the conclusion that the event of Christ is not a "mythical" event at all, at least in the sense in which he himself defines and uses the term "myth." He believes if one takes seriously the way in which the New Testament itself presents the salvation-event of cross and resurrection, there can be no doubt that its affirmation of this event alone as making authentic existence factually possible is not a mythological affirmation and therefore sets no limit to demythologising the New Testament proclamation.

He allows, to be sure, that Christ as the act of God will undoubtedly be regarded as myth by someone for whom *any* talk of God's acting must of necessity be mythology. But he refuses to concede that such a point of view is the only alternative. "I deny," he writes, "that the Christian confession is absolutely myth for man. In any case, it is not myth for the modern man in the specific sense in which I speak of the myth of the New Testament. That it runs up against his opposition even when it is demythologised and and speaks of God's act and man's sin only in a demythologised form (and that he may by all means exploit a well-worn use of language and call it myth) is another matter. It has its basis not in the fact that the Christian confession is myth, but in the fact that it is σκάνδαλον."[213] In other words, Bultmann not only denies the event of Christ is a mythical event ; he also gives a negative answer to the larger question of whether any speaking about God and his action must not by its very nature be mythological. Provided one strictly adheres to *his* sense of the word "myth,"

---

[212] Cf. *Kerygma und Mythos*, i, pp. 47 f. (p. 43); also *Kerygma und Mythos*, ii, p. 206 (p. 210).

[213] *Kerygma und Mythos*, i, pp. 123 f. (p. 104).

he maintains that one can directly speak of the saving act of God and yet do so in a non-mythological way.

To understand how Bultmann can take this position, we must give attention to one of the most unillumined aspects of his thought. In the programmatic essay itself, this question is left quite obscure, and one can therefore appreciate why he has been so generally misunderstood. Nevertheless, in subsequent replies to his critics, Bultmann has given some indication of why he can take such a position by making a distinction between "myth" and "analogy." Since, in spite of its importance for understanding his views, this distinction has been all but universally overlooked,[214] it is necessary to quote at length the passage in which he introduces it.

> One can probably say that what lies behind all of the objections against demythologising is the fear that its consistent execution would make it impossible to speak of God's action or that such speaking would be admissible only as a symbolic way of designating subjective experiences. For is it not mythology to speak of God's act as an objective occurrence that encounters me ?
>
> To this it may be replied at once that if speaking about God's act is to be meaningful, *it must indeed be not simply a figurative or "symbolic" kind of speaking*, but must rather intend a divine act in the fully real and "objective" sense. If, however, it is also not permitted to understand God's act as a phenomenon in the world that can be perceived apart from an *existentiell* encounter with it, then his act can be spoken of only if at the same time I myself as the one who is encountered by it am also spoken of. *To speak*

[214] The sole exception among English-speaking interpreters seems to be Ronald W. Hepburn in his essay in Antony Flew and Alasdair Macintyre (eds.), *New Essays in Philosophical Theology*, London: S.C.M. Press, Ltd., 1955, pp. 229 f. and 237. Because, however, Hepburn makes the fatal mistake of assuming that "Bultmann's first definition of 'myth' [gives] the word a sense sufficiently extended to include every kind of oblique language," he makes the groundless charge that Bultmann's distinction between "analogy" and "myth" is "a procedure for which his definition [*sic* of myth] gives no warrant."

*of God's act means to speak at the same time of my own exist-
ence.* Since human life is a life in space and time, man's
encounter with God must be an event that takes place concretely here and now. Accordingly, what is meant by
speaking of God's act is this event of being addressed,
questioned, judged, and blessed here and now by God.

Therefore, to speak of God's act is not to speak figuratively
or symbolically, but *analogically.* For in such speaking, we
represent God's act as analogous to human action, and we
represent the communion between God and man as
analogous to the communion of men with one another.

Still, the meaning of such speaking must be further
clarified. Mythological thinking represents the divine
action . . . as an action that breaks into and disrupts the
continuum of natural, historical, or psychical events—in
short, as a "miracle." In so doing, it objectifies the divine
action and projects it on to the plane of worldly occurrences.
In truth, however, . . . an act of God is not visible to the
objectifying eye and cannot be demonstrated in the manner
of worldly events. The idea of the unworldliness and
transcendence of the divine action is only preserved when
such action is represented not as something that takes place
between worldly occurrences, but rather as something that
takes place *in* them, so that the closed continuum of worldly
events that presents itself to the objectifying eye remains
untouched. God's act is hidden to every eye but that of
faith. The only thing generally visible and demonstrable is
the "natural" occurrence. It is in it that God's hidden action
takes place.[215]

Two things are made clear by this passage. First, Bultmann
rejects the view that any speaking of God's act must be mythological; and, second, he justifies his rejection by distinguishing
between a "mythological" and an "analogical" manner of
speaking of the divine action. What he appears to mean by

[215] *Kerygma und Mythos,* II, pp. 196 f. (pp. 196 f.).

this distinction, though unfortunately the details of his argument are not completely clear, is that the latter kind of speaking represents God's action in terms of "analogies" drawn from existential analysis, and thus speaks of it quite differently from myth. Whereas in a mythological manner of speaking, God's act is represented objectively as an event between or alongside the other events in the continuum of worldly occurrences, in an analogical manner of speaking, it is represented as objectively "hidden" and, like personal acts in general, discernible only by one who opens himself to it in faith and love.

This interpretation is borne out by the somewhat different version of the same line of argument in *Jesus Christ and Mythology*, although there, too, much is to be desired in the way of completeness and clarity of presentation. Bultmann tells us that "to speak of God as acting involves the events of personal existence" and that "God is a personal being acting on persons."[216] He also says that in our perception of God's act, "the principle is the same as in our personal relationship as persons with persons. Trust in a friend can rest solely on the personality of my friend which I can perceive only when I trust him. There cannot be any trust or love without risk."[217]

It seems legitimate to conclude, then, that what makes it possible for Bultmann to deny that all speaking of God must be mythological is that in the case of God, no less than in that of man, there is a non-mythological conceptuality in which the theologian is able to speak. By representing God in terms of "analogies" based on existential analysis, he can speak of God's act directly and in "the fully real and 'objective' sense," and yet at the same time not objectify it in the misleading manner of myth. For so far from being represented as one objective happening alongside others, which can be perceived apart from any alteration in the perceiver's understanding of his existence, an act of God understood by existential analogy is a fully personal act objectively hidden and perceivable only

[216] *Jesus Christ and Mythology*, pp. 68 and 70.   [217] *Ibid.*, pp. 72 f.

where there is a corresponding change in the self-understanding of the perceiver. Thus, to speak of the historical event of the proclamation of Jesus Christ as God's saving act means that, analogously to the way in which our human words and deeds provide the occasion for personal communion among ourselves, the word that is spoken in Jesus Christ is the means whereby God establishes communion with us all.

But this implies that the act of God as such is only hiddenly present in the historical figure of Jesus or the human word of proclamation in which he is again and again represented. Just as our own personal acts of trust and love are never simply identical with the words and deeds in which they are outwardly expressed, so also is the act of God only "paradoxically" present in the event of Jesus Christ and the proclamation of the church. This is the thought that comes to expression in the concluding sentences of the programmatic essay:

In stripping [the salvation-occurrence] of its mythological garment and presenting it as a historical [*geschichtliches*] occurrence in space and time, we have simply tried to follow the intention of the New Testament and to bring fully into its own *the paradox of its proclamation*—the paradox, namely, that God's eschatological emissary is a concrete historical man, that his eschatological act takes place in a human destiny, that therefore it is an occurrence that cannot be proven in a worldly way to be the eschatological event. . . . It is just because [it] cannot be proven, however, that the Christian proclamation is insured against the charge of being mythology. The transcendence of God is not made immanent as in myth, but the paradox of the transcendent God's presence in history is affirmed: "the word became flesh."[218]

Bultmann is well aware that men to-day will on the whole be just as little disposed as those of every other age to overcome this paradox by appropriating in faith the judgment and

[218] *Kerygma und Mythos*, I, p. 48 (pp. 43 f.).

grace it imports. He is also aware, as a statement already quoted has indicated, that even when this paradox is demythologised and presented solely in existential terms, it may still be dismissed as "mythology" by those who are unwilling to submit to its claim against all their efforts at self-contrived security. Nevertheless, he is convinced that, so far from standing in the way of a consistent demythologisation, *this paradox is precisely what makes such interpretation so necessary.* For only when it is interpreted not as an objective event of the past, but as a personal appeal addressed to our present self-understanding is its true significance fully disclosed.

An Immanent Criticism of Bultmann's Proposal

7. THE EMERGING CONSENSUS

If the attempt of the preceding chapter has been successful, two things should now be evident : (1) Bultmann's theology rests on a clear grasp of the contemporary theological problem, which Bultmann is concerned to solve ; (2) the solution he proposes in his project of existential interpretation may fairly claim to be adequate in the sense of comprising the major dimensions of a comprehensive solution. We have sought to show that the inner unity of Bultmann's thought lies in his contention that the criticism of the New Testament arising with necessity out of the situation of modern man is identical with a criticism sanctioned by the New Testament message itself, and that, in attempting to carry out such criticism, Bultmann has succeeded in presenting the main ingredients of a complete constructive theology.

What must be considered now is whether Bultmann's proposal is adequate when judged in terms of the further criterion of logical self-consistency. To be sure, we have already anticipated our answer to this question by indicating in Chapter 1 that it is with respect to this final test that Bultmann's theology is less than a maximally significant resource. Still, what remains to be done is to justify our answer by exhibiting in a convincing way the inconsistency of his proposed solution.

An Immanent Criticism of Bultmann's Proposal

Before doing this, we must give attention to a matter having a direct bearing on our thesis. Although the question of consistency is unconditionally relevant and would have to be asked of Bultmann's proposal in any event, certain conditions arising from the larger discussion of his work make it an especially pressing question.

Perhaps the "demythologising debate's" most striking characteristic is the substantial agreement among its various participants that Bultmann's proposal is intrinsically problematic. So much agreement is there, in fact, that we may appropriately speak of an emerging consensus that Bultmann's solution is inherently inadequate. From responsible voices on practically every side, the claim has come that his theology is structurally inconsistent and therefore open to the most serious criticism.

Because this is so, it seems only fitting that the present attempt to evaluate his proposal should give consideration to these other criticisms. In addition to placing our argument in its proper setting within the larger discussion of Bultmann's work, such a procedure also offers the advantage of enabling us to deal at least summarily with this larger discussion.

At the risk of a certain oversimplification, the statement may be made that only three distinct positions or types of position have thus far been represented in the demythologising debate. There is, first of all, the "centre" position of Bultmann himself and the others who have allied themselves with him. Among the latter, the most significant voices are those of Bultmann's long-time friend, Friedrich Gogarten, the brilliant team of Christian Hartlich and Walter Sachs, and Hans Werner Bartsch, the editor of the now five-volume series, *Kerygma und Mythos*.[1]

[1] Gogarten's main contribution is his polemical defence of Bultmann, *Entmythologisierung und Kirche*, Stuttgart: Friedrich Vorwerk Verlag, 2nd ed., 1953 (English translation by N. H. Smith in Friedrich Gogarten, *Demythologising and History*, London: S.C.M. Press, Ltd., 1955). The several essays of Hartlich and Sachs, which Bultmann spoke of in 1952 as "the best things written," are unfortunately only partially available in H. W. Bartsch (ed.),

Second, there is what we may describe as the position of the "right," which counts among its representatives not only the Continental Roman Catholic contributors to the discussion,[2] but also the conservative theologians of the German Evangelical Church[3] and Karl Barth and those who share his general point of view.[4] (In grouping together in this way three

---

Kerygma und Mythos, Vol. II, Hamburg: Herbert Reich-Evangelischer Verlag, 1952, pp. 113-149. Among Bartsch's many statements, the most important are (1) the essays in *Kerygma und Mythos*, II, pp. 29-35 and H. W. Bartsch (ed.), *Kerygma und Mythos*, Vol. III, Hamburg: Herbert Reich-Evangelischer Verlag, 1954, pp. 63-79; (2) the Foreword to H. W. Bartsch (ed.), *Kerygma und Mythos*, Vol. V, Hamburg: Herbert Reich-Evangelischer Verlag, 1955, pp. 5-8; and (3) the supplement to *Kerygma und Mythos*, I and II, *Die gegenwärtige Stand der Entmythologisierungsdebatte*, Hamburg: Herbert Reich-Evangelischer Verlag, 1954.

[2] In addition to *Kerygma und Mythos*, V, which contains representative shorter contributions by Catholic theologians, three books are particularly important: Heinrich Fries, *Bultmann, Barth, und die katholische Theologie*, Stuttgart: Schwabenverlag, 1955; René Marlé, S.J., *Bultmann et l'interpretation du Nouveau Testament*, Aubier: Editions Montaigne, 1956; and L. Malevez, *The Christian Message and Myth*, trans. by Olive Wyon, London: S.C.M. Press, Ltd., 1958. We may also mention here the book by the Waldensian theologian, Giovanni Miegge, *Gospel and Myth in the Theology of Rudolf Bultmann*, trans. by Stephen Neill, Richmond: John Knox Press, 1960.

[3] Cf. Ernst Kinder (ed.), *Ein Wort lutherischer Theologie zur Entmythologisierung*, Munich: Evangelischer Pressverband für Bayern, 1952.

[4] In addition to Barth's *Rudolf Bultmann: Ein Versuch, ihn zu verstehen*, Zollikon-Zürich: Evangelischer Verlag, 2nd ed., 1953, cf. the section from *Kirchliche Dogmatik* reprinted in *Kerygma und Mythos*, II, pp. 102-109. From the extensive literature by other representatives of the general "Barthian" position, we may select as of paramount importance Heinrich Ott, *Geschichte und Heilsgeschichte in der Theologie Rudolf Bultmanns*, Tübingen: J. C. B. Mohr, 1955; and also Ott's essay in H. W. Bartsch (ed.), *Kerygma und Mythos*, Vol. IV, Hamburg: Herbert Reich-Evangelischer Verlag, 1955, pp. 107-131. To this, then, may be added: two essays by Markus Barth: "Die Methode von Bultmanns 'Theologie des Neuen Testaments,'" *Theologische Zeitschrift*, January-February, 1955, pp. 1-27, and "Introduction to Demythologising," *Journal of Religion*, July, 1957, pp. 145-155; Emil Brunner, *The Christian Doctrine of Creation and Redemption*, trans. by Olive Wyon, Philadelphia: The Westminster Press, 1952, pp. 263-270; and the essays by Helmut Thielicke in H. W. Bartsch (ed.), *Kerygma und Mythos*, Vol. I, Hamburg: Herbert Reich-Evangelischer Verlag, 2nd ed., 1951, pp. 159-189 (English translation by R. H. Fuller in H. W. Bartsch [ed.], *Kerygma and Myth*, New York: Harper Torchbooks, 1961, pp. 138-174), and *Expository Times*, February, March, 1956, pp. 154-157, 175-177.

so ostensibly different standpoints, we may appear to have overleaped the bounds of legitimate simplification and to be guilty of serious injustice to one or more of the parties concerned. In defence, however, we may say simply that *with respect to the one issue under discussion*, namely, the validity of Bultmann's programme of demythologisation and existential interpretation, there seems to be no difference whatever between the three points of view. Their reactions to Bultmann's proposal are in general identical, and the grounds to which they appeal in criticising it are one and the same.[5] We may also include as representative of the "right" several of the English-speaking contributors to the discussion ; for example, Ian Henderson and John Macquarrie, to whose works we have already frequently referred,[6] Austin Farrer,[7] Arthur Smethurst,[8] and Geraint Vaughan Jones.[9] Minor differences aside, these Anglo-Saxon theologians agree with their Continental counterparts among the Catholics, the "orthodox," and the "Barthians" in rejecting Bultmann's proposal as making impossible an adequate restatement of the Christian message.

Finally, there is a third and decidedly minority point of view somewhere to the "left" of the hypothetical Bultmannian

[5] Bultmann himself has pointed this out in *Glauben und Verstehen*, Vol. III, Tübingen: J. C. B. Mohr, 1960, p. 179; and it may be readily confirmed by a comparative reading of (1) Barth's *Rudolf Bultmann: Ein Versuch, ihn zu verstehen*; (2) Ernst Kinder (ed.), *op. cit.*; and (3) *Kerygma und Mythos*, v, Cf. also Heinrich Fries, *op. cit.*; H. W. Bartsch, *Die gegenwärtige Stand der Entmythologisierungsdebatte*, pp. 40 ff.; and Schubert M. Ogden, "The Debate on 'Demythologising,' " *Journal of Bible and Religion*, January, 1959, pp. 25 and 27, n. 23.

[6] Cf. *Myth in the New Testament*, London: S.C.M. Press, Ltd., 1952; and *An Existentialist Theology: A Comparison of Heidegger and Bultmann*, London: S.C.M. Press, Ltd., 1955.

[7] Cf. "An English Appreciation" in H. W. Bartsch (ed.), *Kerygma and Myth*, New York: Harper Torchbooks, 1961, pp. 212-223.

[8] Cf. *Modern Science and Christian Beliefs*, New York: Abingdon Press, 1955, pp. 281-287.

[9] Cf. *Christology and Myth in the New Testament*, New York: Harper & Brothers, 1956.

"centre." The most articulate spokesman for this position has been the Basel systematic theologian Fritz Buri. In attempting to make explicit the dogmatic implications of Albert Schweitzer's thesis of "consistent eschatology," Buri has made use of the resources of Karl Jaspers' existential philosophy and so has developed a theology similar to Bultmann's. Nevertheless, as his contributions to the discussion over demythologising make clear, he rejects Bultmann's position as simply one more attempt to evade the implications of the "delayed parousia."[10]

As we have already indicated, the striking thing about the alternatives to Bultmann's position is that, for all of their differences, they agree completely at a crucial point in their criticisms. From both the "right" and the "left," responsible critics have repeatedly charged that Bultmann's view is, strictly speaking, not *a* view at all, but an uneasy synthesis of two different and ultimately incompatible standpoints. Of course, there have been those who were more interested in accepting or rejecting Bultmann's proposal than in understanding it ; and it is hardly surprising that they have tended to obscure its ambiguity by their precipitant yeas or nays. Nevertheless, wherever the task of understanding has been taken seriously, whether by the "right" or by the "left," there has been a marked tendency to conclude that Bultmann's theology is structurally inconsistent, and so may be neither simply affirmed nor simply denied.

In order to give evidence of this consensus and to clarify its bearing on our own critical analysis, we propose to examine at length two of the representative contributions to the larger discussion.

The first contribution is that by Karl Barth, particularly as presented in his book, *Rudolf Bultmann : Ein Versuch, ihn zu*

---

[10] Cf. "Das Problem der ausgebliebenen Parusie," *Schweizerische theologische Umschau*, October-December, 1946, pp. 97-120; "Theologie und Philosophie," *Theologische Zeitschrift*, March-April, 1952, pp. 116-134; and *Kerygma und Mythos*, II, pp. 85-101.

verstehen. As is clear already from the title, Barth's concern is primarily to understand Bultmann's proposal. He believes that an attempt at understanding is imperative if there is to be any break in the stalemate that has gradually arisen in the discussion of Bultmann's work. Because Bultmann's friends as well as his enemies have pretended to more of an understanding of his thought than they actually possess, the debate has come to a standstill. Therefore, before one can take sides either with Bultmann or against him, he must try simply to understand him.[11]

Barth suggests that a good way to begin is to recognise that two tendencies appear to define the direction of Bultmann's undertaking. First of all, he seems intent on "understanding the New Testament as the document of a *message* (kerygma, proclamation, sermon)"—and, indeed, as Barth adds, "as that and only that !"[12] Second, his primary concern appears to be to translate this message from the antiquated conceptuality of the New Testament into a form understandable and relevant to men to-day.

But already, Barth holds, one can hardly feel certain he has understood Bultmann's proposal. For while his intention to interpret the New Testament as essentially message is understandable, his further assumption that what is presented in the kerygma is an *existentiell* self-understanding is much less so.[13] Likewise, although one may readily grant that the task of translation is a perennially important task for any responsible theology, it is difficult to understand how this concern can be made the *cura prior* that Bultmann seems to make it. For in relation to theology's primary responsibility to understand the message itself, the work of translating it must always be at best a *cura posterior*.[14]

The difficulty here is not lessened when one gives attention to the supposed origins of Bultmann's thought in the two

[11] Cf. *op. cit.*, pp. 3 f.   [12] *Ibid.*, p. 4.
[13] Cf. *ibid.*, p. 6.   [14] Cf. *ibid.*, pp. 7 f.

movements of form-criticism and the return to Reformation theology.[15] Although it is easy to see how each of these movements might account for Bultmann's preoccupation with the idea of kerygma, one cannot understand how either of them could explain his inordinate concern with the task of translation. As a matter of fact, Barth suggests, the more likely source of this concern is the characteristic interest of the great liberal theologians. In any case, it is impossible to understand how Bultmann can picture himself as standing in the tradition of the Reformation, especially of Luther, and yet at the same time give the matter of translation a weight assigned it only by the anti- or at least un-Reformation theology of the last two hundred years.[16]

After these introductory remarks about the direction of Bultmann's programme, Barth undertakes to summarise and appraise the results of Bultmann's exegesis. He maintains that the basic conception in Bultmann's interpretation is that the kerygma essentially discloses "*a double determination of man* : an old determination of his existence in which he finds himself exposed by the kerygma and a new one to which he finds himself called by it."[17] Then, together with these determinations, Bultmann speaks of "*something that determines man* : God's saving act, which is known and experienced in faith and takes place in the transition from the one determination of existence to the other."[18]

According to Barth, this logical sequence of, first, man's experience of himself both as he is and as he ought to be and, second, the act of God that makes the transition from the one to the other possible constantly recurs in Bultmann's writings and may therefore be presumed to be important for understanding them. But by the same token, he thinks, one must raise the most serious question about the adequacy of Bult-

---

[15] Cf. the joint statement by the Tübingen theological faculty, *Für und wider die Theologie Bultmanns*, Tübingen: J. C. B. Mohr, 3rd ed., 1952, pp. 16 ff.
[16] Cf. *op. cit.*, pp. 9 ff.   [17] *Ibid.*, p. 12.   [18] *Ibid.*

mann's translation of the New Testament. "Does the message of the New Testament also begin with an explication of the man who experiences himself as its hearer ? Are its statements concerning God's saving act for man . . . also first presented in the form of statements about his own self-experience ?"[19]

Barth argues that there is in fact a fateful reversal of the New Testament order of priorities in Bultmann's translation. In what seems to be a characteristically Lutheran concern to understand christology and soteriology as a unity (*Hoc est Christus cognoscere* : *beneficia eius cognoscere*), Bultmann forgets that this unity must always be understood as a "unity of differences" in which christology is the prior and determining element, and in effect dissolves christology by presenting the Christ-event as hardly more than a postulate of the doctrine of salvation.[20] This is clear, Barth believes, both from Bultmann's interpretation of man's twofold possibility of existence and from his presentation of the occurrence of Christ.

By interpreting man's existence outside faith and in faith as *existentiell* possibilities discoverable by philosophy apart from Christ, Bultmann seems to deprive the Christ-event of all independent significance. Instead of the New Testament view that what has occurred in Christ is "completely new," he presents us with the thought that Christ is simply the historical occasion through which man's natural self-understanding is radicalised and corrected and thereby thrust upon him as a summons to decision.[21] This impression is confirmed by the way in which Bultmann understands Jesus Christ. For notwithstanding his emphasis on the uniqueness and indispensability of this event, he never succeeds in making clear that it is anything other than the shadowy and indeterminable "whence" of the transition from inauthentic to authentic existence.[22]

In other words, Bultmann not only fails to express the Christ-

---

[19] *Ibid.*, p. 13.   [20] Cf. *ibid.*, pp. 12 f. and 17 f.
[21] Cf. *ibid.*, pp. 14 ff.   [22] Cf. *ibid.*, p. 18.

event as "an event significant in itself"—*extra nos, sine nobis, et contra nos*; he even seems to hold that its "significance must, as it were, first accrue to it by reason of its entrance into the kerygma and into the obedience of faith of the kerygma's hearers."[23] Thus the kerygma, as he understands it, is not so much a testimony to a saving event outside of, and prior to, it as it is simply another way—and finally the *only* way—of speaking of this event itself.[24]

Similarly, Barth argues, what Bultmann means by "faith" is less a response in which one appropriates what God has *already* done in Christ crucified and risen than it is an attitude in which the crucifixion and resurrection themselves first take place. Consequently, one is driven to ask whether the kerygma as Bultmann understands it is really a "gospel" at all or simply a "new law." Its significance seems to be completely exhausted in laying on man the *demand* that he permit himself to be crucified with Christ in order to rise with him to new life.[25]

In short, Barth maintains it is practically impossible to recognise the New Testament's own idiom and accent in Bultmann's interpretation of its message. Like many another Lutheran before him—Barth mentions, among others, the young Luther, Melanchthon, Ritschl, and the Ritschlians—Bultmann succeeds in avoiding a one-sided objectivism only by falling, or appearing to fall, into a subjectivism equally one-sided.[26] Barth thinks this still must be said even though the emphasis Bultmann places on the event of Christ "should be overlooked neither by the opponents nor the over-zealous friends of his conception."

That he intends to bring to expression and to do justice not only to Paul, but also to the entire New Testament is unmistakable. So also is the fact that to-day, when he is seen, say, from the standpoint of Karl Jaspers and his theological disciple, Fritz Buri, he willingly incurs the same condem-

---

[23] *Ibid.*, p. 20.   [24] Cf. *ibid.*, p. 17.
[25] Cf. *ibid.*, pp. 18 f.   [26] Cf. *ibid.*, pp. 12 f.

nation and makes himself guilty of the same scandal as the rest of us. Therefore, so far as concerns his *intention*, which thus becomes visible, he is to be explained by neither an older nor a more recent liberalism. If only this intention were also so visible in the actual *carrying out of it* that it could not be misunderstood! If only he would speak of the cross and resurrection of Jesus Christ in such a way that the emphasis he actually places on them and on the Christ-occurrence in general would seem *justified*! It does not seem to me to be so justified that I must not concede a certain justice to the criticism Bultmann has experienced at this point from both the right and the left. All of which I do, however, only with a heavy heart.[27]

Having thus stated what he has understood of Bultmann's theology and what seems to him to be its weakness, Barth devotes the remainder of his analysis to a threefold task.

First, he undertakes to consider demythologisation and existential interpretation as the *method* whereby the results he has already discussed are obtained. His point here is that it is precisely the employment of this method that makes it impossible for Bultmann to express the New Testament's emphasis on God's act in Jesus Christ and also accounts for the fateful reversal in which soteriology replaces christology as the prior and determining factor.[28] "Bultmann is loved and praised," Barth writes, "because at least at this one point [*sic* of the indispensability of the event Jesus Christ], and to the chagrin of Fritz Buri, he breaks out of the existentialist scheme. But he himself has raised the question whether this is compatible with the programme of demythologisation, and I do not see he has ever satisfactorily answered it. At any rate, it is certain that, in spite of this noteworthy inconsistency, what he has

[27] *Ibid.*, pp. 23 f.
[28] Cf. *ibid.*, pp. 32-41. Elsewhere, Barth argues that "we have every occasion in specific contexts to speak 'mythically' and to do so with a good conscience, since if we were to 'demythologise' in an all too basic sense, we would no longer be able to bear witness to Jesus Christ" (*Kerygma und Mythos*, II, p. 108).

done to the New Testament message in the name of existentialism makes it extremely difficult, if not impossible, to recognise it in his presentation."[29]

Second, Barth attempts to fix more exactly than he has previously done the relevant historical categories for understanding Bultmann's proposal. This he does by first considering the possibilities that most naturally come to mind ; for example, that Bultmann is a radical modernist of the stamp of Strauss, an apologist like Schleiermacher, a historian in the grand manner of the nineteenth century, or simply an existentialist philosopher. Against each of these, Barth raises certain objections and suggests as a more likely alternative that Bultmann is to be understood "simply as a *Lutheran*—although, of course, a Lutheran *sui generis*."[30] To be sure, Barth acknowledges that even this interpretation can hardly be regarded as exhaustive. Yet he concludes this part of his discussion with the warning that "whoever strikes out at Bultmann had better be careful he does not accidentally hit Luther, who 'in some way or other' is also on the field in him !"[31]

Finally, Barth presents a summary criticism of Bultmann's proposal by contrasting it with his own constructive position on the underlying hermeneutical problem. He argues, first, that Bultmann's general theory of understanding as necessarily presupposing a "pre-understanding," which is then conceived existentially, makes an adequate interpretation of the New Testament impossible ; and, second, that, so far from being the application of a general hermeneutical principle, exegesis of the Scriptures is unique and so has to take place by means of its own distinctive method.[32]

According to Barth, the most disturbing thing about Bultmann's proposal is not its "massive anti-supernaturalist negations" or even its forced interpretations, but "the pre-Copernican behaviour" evidently underlying them. In insisting on "the obligatory 'pre-understanding' " and "the binding

[29] *Ibid.*, p. 40.   [30] *Ibid.*, p. 46.   [31] *Ibid.*, p. 48.   [32] Cf. *ibid.*, pp. 48-52.

world-picture," Bultmann seems bent on reversing the last thirty years of theological development by leading theology back into the "Egyptian captivity" of an alien philosophy.[33] Thus, Barth's final criticism of Bultmann (for which, strangely enough, the reader is hardly prepared by the earlier remarks about Bultmann's "intention" and the attempt to fix his place in the history of theology) is that, in his obsessive and one-sided concern to translate the kerygma for the modern man, Bultmann represents a kind of throwback to the liberal era of Ritschl, Harnack, and Troeltsch. At any rate, this appears to be the burden of the maze of mixed metaphors and cryptic remarks with which Barth's analysis closes.

Before proceeding to consideration of the second contribution we may summarise Barth's argument in the following theses :

1. Bultman's theology, as it now stands, is marked by the "noteworthy inconsistency" that the emphasis it rightly places on the centrality and indispensability of the event Jesus Christ is not justified by the interpretation it gives of this event.

2. The underlying cause of this inconsistency is that the method of Bultmann's theology in its negative and positive aspects (i.e., as demythologisation and existential interpretation), is in principle incapable of bringing such emphasis to expression.

3. The only tenable alternative to Bultmann's position, then, is a theology that rejects or at least qualifies his proposed method in favour of a special biblical hermeneutic and, by so doing, frees itself to justify its emphasis on the Christ-event by means of statements that (from Bultmann's point of view) are essentially mythological and unamenable to existential interpretation.

If one of the weaknesses of Barth's contribution is that it sometimes gives the impression of unduly simplifying the complex motives of Bultmann's proposal, one of the strengths of the contribution of Fritz Buri is that it gives no such impres-

[33] Cf. *ibid.*, pp. 53 f.

sion. Buri clearly recognises in a way Barth does not that Bultmann is quite as much concerned to be a modern man and to face responsibly the demands arising from that situation as he is to be an obedient servant of the church's proclamation or a continuator of Lutheran theology. Consequently, in his attempt to understand Bultmann's programme, Buri is not embarrassed by finally drawing a conclusion that seems obscured rather than clarified by a one-sided estimation of Bultmann's "intention." On the contrary, he makes completely clear that the inconsistency of Bultmann's position is already implicit in the incompatible concerns underlying it.

This viewpoint is presented in detail in the essay, "Entmythologisierung oder Entkerygmatisierung der Theologie," which is the classic statement of Buri's contribution to the discussion.[34] He argues that Bultmann's theology is best understood as an attempt to respond to three necessities regarded as determinative for the contemporary theological situation.

First, because of modern man's understanding of himself and his world, there is the necessity of freeing the Christian message from the New Testament mythology. Second, there is the need for an existential interpretation of this mythology, which Bultmann considers justified because it is the nature of myth, both formally and materially, to require such interpretation. Third, the demythologisation and existential interpretation thus demanded must be so carried out that the kerygma is not eliminated but preserved.

According to Buri, Bultmann is just as insistent that the New Testament message not be deprived of its "kerygma character" as that every attempt to perpetuate its mythology be rejected. Hence his demand for a "demythologising interpretation" that can disclose "the truth of the kerygma as kerygma for the man who no longer thinks mythologically."[35]

Buri next points out that the result of Bultmann's effort to

---

[34] Cf. *Kerygma und Mythos*, II, pp. 85-101.
[35] Cf. *ibid.*, pp. 85 ff.; cf. *Kerygma und Mythos*, I, p. 26 (p. 15).

meet this demand is a theology having three defining characteristics. First, it involves a "complete destruction of the traditional Christian conception of *Heilsgeschichte*."[36] Insofar as this conception consists of objective statements about saving events supposed to have happened independently of our own understanding and decision, then, for Bultmann, it is simply a myth no longer credible or relevant. Second, however, Bultmann's theology provides a kind of "substitute" for the objective history of salvation by its existential interpretation of the Christian understanding of existence. As Buri puts it, "What is finished as objective statement now becomes significant as the expression of a possibility for man's self-understanding."[37] Finally, Bultmann's theology repudiates a "Christianity without Christ" such as might appear to be implied by its existential interpretation, and places the greatest possible emphasis on God's saving act in Jesus of Nazareth. In an obvious effort to avoid the elimination of the kerygma that was the outcome of earlier attempts at demythologising, Bultmann "recurs" to the event of Christ as constituting a decisive difference between Christian faith and theology and the "natural" self-understanding clarified by philosophy.[38]

This forces Bultmann to ask, however, whether he has not set a limit to what he has previously presented as an unlimited demand for demythologisation and existential interpretation. Buri's contention is that the only answer Bultmann has a right to give is affirmative. It seems clear to him that when Bultmann "suddenly appeals to God's saving act in Christ as the ground for the possibility of Christian self-understanding," he is guilty of "an untenable turning aside from the radical consequences of his demythologisation thesis."[39]

In Buri's judgment, existential interpretation inevitably leads to the same kind of dissolution of the specific possibility

---

[36] *Kerygma und Mythos*, II, p. 88.   [37] *Ibid.*   [38] Cf. *ibid.*, p. 90.
[39] *Ibid.*, p. 91 and "Das Problem der ausgebliebenen Parusie," *Schweizerische theologische Umschau*, October-December, 1946, p. 117.

of Christian existence into a general possibility of man as such as was the result of earlier attempts at demythologisation— although not in the sense of German idealism or a mystical concept of religion, but in the sense of existential philosophy.[40] Therefore, when Bultmann appeals against the claims of philosophy to the unique event of Jesus Christ, Buri holds this is a "falling back into mythology" and a "contradiction of [Bultmann's] own presuppositions."[41] In this sense, he draws the conclusion that the incompatible needs to which Bultmann tries to respond give rise to "a mongrel thing that can neither satisfy a myth-believing theology of the history of salvation nor stand up before the self-understanding of contemporary philosophy."[42]

Buri seeks to support this conclusion in the second section of his essay, where he argues that Bultmann's theology runs into three fundamental "difficulties." The implication, though this is never stated, is that each of these difficulties is but an expression of the one underlying *Problematik*.

Buri points out, first, that Bultmann's attempt to distinguish his interpretation of the kerygma from existential philosophy discloses an ambiguous and, in fact, self-contradictory under- standing of man's "fallenness." So long as he is speaking constructively in terms of his existential interpretation, Bult- mann represents fallenness as a possibility of historical existence for which man decides by choosing to understand himself in a certain way. As soon, however, as he tries to deny to the natural man the possibility of moving from fallenness to authenticity, he in effect abandons this understanding and reverts to a mythological view of fallenness as a natural state or condition. This is evident, Buri believes, because it is only of such a non-historical condition that one can say what Bult- mann says about fallenness, namely, that knowledge of it,

---

[40] Cf. *Kerygma und Mythos*, II, pp. 89 and 92.   [41] *Ibid.*, p. 91.
[42] "Theologie und Philosophie," *Theologische Zeitschrift*, March-April, 1952, p. 129.

which he readily grants to the natural man, in no sense constitutes a way out of it. If fallenness were really an inauthentic self-understanding, then knowledge of it would already be "the beginning of a new and authentic self-understanding."[43] Therefore, since Bultmann concedes that the natural man has such knowledge, he can avoid the obvious implication only by giving up his existential interpretation of man's fallen state.[44]

An equally serious difficulty arises when Bultmann tries to distinguish his position from a traditional theology of the history of salvation. In order to avoid the charge that his appeal to the event of Christ is a relapse into myth, Bultmann is compelled so to interpret this event that "the kerygma of God's saving act threatens to dissolve into a mere human self-understanding."[45] Buri holds that Bultmann's presentation of Christ in terms of his "existential significance" involves a complete dehistoricisation in which the New Testament's statements concerning the cross and the resurrection are reduced to dispensable mythological expressions of authentic self-understanding. This is so, he argues, because Bultmann's theory of myth as the expression of self-understanding is incapable of doing justice to the meaning of myth for its original adherents. Although for us to-day, this theory provides the only way in which mythological statements can be understood and appropriated, "one who believes in myth knows nothing of 'myth's true intention' as Bultmann understands it."[46] This is particularly true of the earliest Christian community. "However strange it may seem to us, the man of the New Testament does not experience the reality of salvation in an existentially interpretable word that proclaims God's love and reconciliation, but rather in Jesus' atoning sacrifice and in his resurrection, which brings about the inauguration

[43] *Kerygma und Mythos*, II, p. 93.
[44] Cf. *ibid.*, pp. 93 f.; cf. also "Theologie und Philosophie," *Theologische Zeitschrift*, March-April, 1952, p. 125.
[45] *Kerygma und Mythos*, II, p. 91.   [46] *Ibid.*, p. 94.

of the world of God. What appears to us to be mythology is for him not an expression of his self-understanding, but rather is assumed to be the actual occurrence on which his self-understanding is based."[47]

To reverse this relation, then, as Bultmann has to do if he is to avoid falling back into myth, is to deprive the event of Christ of any independent significance. Existence in faith dissolves into a general human possibility, and the whole apparatus of cross, resurrection, and kerygma becomes simply a dispensable symbol of this possibility.

The third difficulty Bultmann encounters is revealed by the utter lack of clarity in his treatment of the relation between historical research and the proclamation of the word. On the one hand, he affirms that the kerygma is not interested in historical research and that it would be wrong "to try to justify faith in God's word by historical investigation." On the other hand, he also asserts that the kerygma has its origin in a historical event and that the word of God is "simply the proclamation of the person and destiny of Jesus of Nazareth in their significance as the history of salvation."

According to Buri, however, it is impossible to combine these two assertions in a consistent way. If the content of the kerygma is an actual salvation-occurrence in history, then the kerygma can hardly be independent of historical inquiry or disinterested in it. That Bultmann is forced to conclude otherwise, however, is fully understandable if one recognises the complexity of motives underlying his thought. For "only by disregarding a historical way of looking at things can one still speak of a kerygma on the basis of a saving act of God in Christ. Hence because Bultmann wants to hold on to such a kerygma, he arrives at a theory of the proclamation that is incompatible with historical research."[48]

Much of the force of Buri's argument here turns on the so-called thesis of "consistent eschatology" that he affirms in

[47] *Ibid.,* p. 95.   [48] *Ibid.,* p. 96.

common with Albert Schweitzer and Martin Werner. According to this thesis, the central and all-determining feature of the New Testament is its belief that the historical event Jesus of Nazareth is the beginning of the new age, which is shortly to be consummated by Jesus' return as the apocalyptic Son of Man. Because this expected parousia has never occurred, the whole notion that Jesus is God's eschatological act has been radically called in question by the actual course of history. Therefore, Buri can argue that it is only by adopting a non- or even anti-historical point of view that Bultmann can continue to speak of a salvation-occurrence in Jesus Christ or in the word that proclaims him. Bultmann's "assertion of a historically unknowable eschatological occurrence in the proclamation of the word is only a final substitute for the salvation-occurrence that is proclaimed in the New Testament but never occurred. The kerygma is simply a final remnant of mythology that is inconsistently maintained."[49]

Since the last paragraph gives sufficient indication of Buri's own constructive position, we may conclude our analysis of his contribution by summarising its main points. Here, too, there are three theses :

1. Bultmann's theology in its present form is characterised by the *Problematik* that its ostensibly unlimited demand for demythologisation and existential interpretation, which, as it rightly sees, is unavoidable, is in fact limited by its appeal to an event that is mythological and inexpressible in existential terms.

2. The underlying cause of this *Problematik* is that Bultmann's theology represents an attempt to respond to two mutually incompatible necessities : on the one hand, to do justice to modern man's picture of himself and his world (whence the unavoidable demand for demythologisation and existential interpretation) and, on the other hand, to preserve

---

[49] *Ibid.* Cf. also "Theologie und Philosophie," *Theologische Zeitschrift,* March-April, 1952, p. 128.

the "kerygma character" of the New Testament proclamation (whence the appeal to the mythological saving event of Jesus Christ).

3. The only tenable alternative to Bultmann's position, therefore, is to reject his appeal to a mythological saving-event as incompatible with modern man's picture of himself and his world and, in so doing to carry to its logical conclusion, to the point of "dekerygmatisation," the programme of demythologisation he proposes.

It will be apparent at once that there is a striking parallelism between these three theses of Buri's and the corresponding ones in which we previously summarised the contribution of Karl Barth. Although we have obviously formulated the two sets of theses so as to exhibit this parallelism to the best advantage, there still is an almost shocking amount of agreement between them. With the sole exception of the third theses (and, of course, the corresponding changes they necessitate in each case in the formulation, but not in the substance of the others), Barth and Buri appear to be in complete accord.

Thus it was for good reason that we have spoken of an emerging consensus concerning Bultmann's solution to the theological problem. For though we have by no means documented the full scope of this consensus,[50] we have shown how in the case of representative spokesmen for the two alternatives to his position there is actual unanimity about the structural inconsistency, or inner *Problematik* of his proposal.

But we have also done something more : We have taken the initial step towards an eventual constructive resolution of the theological problem. If it is true, as we shall presently seek to show, that a tenable solution to this problem is not to

---

[50] To do so would be perfunctory. Cf. e.g., the precisely parallel criticisms by Adolf Kolping, *Kerygma und Mythos*, v, pp. 17, 22 f., and 28; L. Malevez, *op. cit.*, pp. 16, 67 ff., and 82; Heinrich Fries, *op. cit.*, p. 162; Markus Barth, "Introduction to Demythologising," *Journal of Religion*, July, 1957, p. 155; Emil Brunner, *op. cit.*, pp. 267 f.; John Macquarrie, *op. cit.*, p. 243; and Helmut Thielicke, *Kerygma und Mythos*, i, p. 173 (p. 154).

be found in Bultmann's proposal, but must rather be sought in one of the two alternatives just considered, then the value of having examined these alternatives as carefully as we have is obvious. Indeed, it was with this in mind that the foregoing analysis has been so fully developed. We have deliberately considered the alternatives to Bultmann's position in sufficient detail to be able readily to subject them to the same kind of criticism his own proposal has received.

Before we attempt such a criticism, however, we must confirm the emerging consensus whose outlines are now before us by exhibiting in a definitive way the inner *Problematik* of Bultmann's theology.

8. THE STRUCTURAL INCONSISTENCY OF BULTMANN'S SOLUTION

The first step in an immanent criticism of Bultmann's proposal is to show that its entire meaning may be reduced to two fundamental propositions: (1) Christian faith is to be interpreted exhaustively and without remainder as man's original possibility of authentic historical (*geschichtlich*) existence as this is more or less adequately clarified and conceptualised by an appropriate philosophical analysis. (2) Christian faith is actually realisable, or is a "possibility in fact," only because of the particular historical (*historisch*) event Jesus of Nazareth, which is the originative event of the church and its distinctive word and sacraments. The second step in the criticism is to demonstrate that, as Barth and Buri and many others have held, these two propositions are mutually incompatible.[51]

That the first proposition relevantly expresses one main facet of Bultmann's thought should be evident as soon as one

---

[51] The reader may wish to compare with this section the parallel criticism that is presented in "Bultmann's Project of Demythologisation and the Problem of Theology and Philosophy," *Journal of Religion*, July, 1957, pp. 164-169.

notes that it simply summarises what is presupposed by his demand for demythologisation and existential interpretation. As we saw in Chapter II, Bultmann regards this demand as justified because the New Testament message itself not only permits but requires just such interpretation. He everywhere assumes that what is at stake in the Christian message is completely independent of the objective truth or falsity of the mythological assertions in which the New Testament authors explicate their faith. This he can do because he also takes for granted that the Christian faith is nothing other than a possibility of *existentiell* self-understanding, which is something entirely different from objective knowledge and assertion.

Furthermore, it is only because this is so that he can assume that the Christian faith may be expressed with complete adequacy by simply using the concepts of Heidegger's existential analysis. Unless he presupposed that the Christian faith is entirely a matter of *existentiell* self-understanding, he could not so consistently argue that it can be expressed without remainder solely in existential terms.

Finally, the implication of such an argument is that the essential content or structure of Christian faith is discoverable simply by man as such, or, at least, by a sufficiently perceptive philosopher. If this were not so, it would be impossible for Bultmann to hold that the conceptuality of existential philosophy provides a completely adequate vehicle for explicating the Christian understanding of existence.

But the first proposition is relevant for reasons other than the presupposition of Bultmann's proposal. Its relevance is also evident from the way in which he carries out his hermeneutical programme. Thus it is clear from his interpretation of the New Testament view of human existence that he understands life in faith to be simply the moment-by-moment realisation of man's original possibility of authentic self-understanding. That this is so is already strongly suggested when he admits the seriousness of the question whether there is really any difference between his own view and that of the existential philosophers. But when he goes on to answer this question as he does, there can hardly be any doubt. He makes clear that, so far as its content is concerned, Christian faith is nothing other than that freedom from the past and openness for the future that is the original possibility of authentic human existence.

Even more impressive, however, is that the same conclusion must also be drawn from the argument in the last major section of the programmatic essay. Although Bultmann emphatically denies that theology and philosophy are identical and insists on the independent significance of the event Jesus Christ, he nevertheless interprets this event in such a way that to believe in it is indistinguishable from an authentic understanding of one's existence as a person. Nor is this simply the unexpressed implication of his demythologisation of the Christ-occurrence. On the contrary, as is evident from Section 6, he explicitly affirms that "the possibility of the word's being understood coincides with the possibility of man's understanding himself."[52] He does not say merely that these possibilities are closely related—say, as ground and consequent[53]—but states that they are one and the same thing. Thus, in one of his most recent essays, he tells us that "genuine proclamation preaches [Jesus] as the end of the world when it preaches him as the Lord. 'Jesus Christ is Lord'—that is the oldest Christian confession. What does this confession mean? *It means to allow the same paradox to apply to one's own life* and, although one lives within the world, . . . to be already freed from it."[54]

What is said here with particular clarity is implicitly affirmed in every sentence of Bultmann's interpretation of the event of

---

[52] *Glauben und Verstehen*, Vol. I, Tübingen: J. C. B. Mohr, 2nd ed., 1954, p. 284.

[53] Cf. John Macquarrie, *op. cit.*, pp. 109, 202.

[54] *Glauben und Verstehen*, III, p. 128; italics added (English translation by H. O. J. Brown in Walter Leibrecht [ed.], *Religion and Culture: Essays in Honour of Paul Tillich*, New York: Harper & Brothers, 1959, p. 241).

Christ. Throughout his writings he makes plain that the christological assertions of the New Testament have a purely existential meaning. So far from being statements concerning an actual historical occurrence (except, of course, insofar as they are objective historical judgments that are subject to scientific criteria and so are irrelevant to faith), such assertions are merely dispensable mythological symbols of a certain understanding of man's existence before God. Thus, on Bultmann's own showing, the demand to believe in the cross as the salvation-event is strictly identical with the demand to surrender one's previous self-understanding and to understand oneself in the moment in an authentic way. Similarly, to believe in the resurrection is simply to accept the possibility of new and authentic existence that is continually present in one's encounters with other persons and with his own destiny.

In other words, Bultmann reduces the entire contents of the traditional Christian confession to one fundamental assertion : *I henceforth understand myself no longer in terms of my past, but solely in terms of the future that is here and now disclosed to me as grace in my encounter with the church's proclamation.* Thus, from the standpoint of existential interpretation, to affirm that Jesus Christ is the pre-existent Son of God, that he was born of the Virgin Mary, that he descended into hell, that on the third day he arose again from the dead, that he now sits at the right hand of the Father from whence he shall eventually come to judge the quick and the dead—in short, to affirm any or all of the church's traditional assertions about Christ is in reality simply to affirm the authentic self-understanding presented in the Christian message. This is the import of all of Bultmann's constructive statements, and it is for this reason we have said that, for him, the Christian faith is to be interpreted exhaustively and without remainder as man's original possibility of authentic existence.

Before turning now to show the relevance of the second proposition, it will be well if we ask ourselves once again what makes it so imperative for Bultmann to affirm the first one. What are the motives that prompt him to insist that Christian faith has to be interpreted solely in existential terms ?

The first such motive, of course, is that this is the only way in which to meet the unavoidable demand of modern man for a demythologised New Testament. As we pointed out in the preceding chapter, Bultmann believes men to-day must inevitably regard the Christian message as irrelevant until its assertions about Jesus Christ are so interpreted as to reveal their independence of the mythological concepts in which they have traditionally been expressed. But this means that such affirmations must be interpreted existentially; for it is only in this way that the complete independence of myth required can be achieved.

The second and even more fundamental motive is that this is the only way the Christian faith itself can find adequate expression. Although, as we have indicated, this point has almost never been appreciated by Bultmann's critics, the key to understanding his proposal is his statement that "demythologisation is a demand of faith itself."[55] What he means is that the true character of the Christian faith as the New Testament understands it becomes clear only when it is interpreted as man's original possibility of authentic existence.

Thus, as we have seen from his discussion with existential philosophy, he readily grants that "faith" and "love" must be a possibility discoverable by man as such on the ground that "Christian existence is nothing mysterious or supernatural."[56] The reason this possibility may not be regarded as "mysterious or supernatural" is that this would competely undercut the New Testament's view of man before God. This is made clear in an argument in which Bultmann tries to show that, in spite of his fallenness, the natural man can have a knowledge

[55] *Kerygma und Mythos*, II, p. 207 (English translation by R. H. Fuller in H. W. Bartsch [ed.], *Kerygma and Myth*, New York: Harper Torchbooks, 1961, p. 210).
[56] *Kerygma und Mythos*, I, p. 36 (p. 27).

of his authentic existence. Precisely in man's fallen decisions, he argues, "man understands what resolution, freedom, and historicity are. And it is just for this reason that faith can say of existence before faith that it stands in hate, in sin. It does not stand in a neutral sphere so that if it is to be moved to love, it must first undergo a miraculous transformation. Love is not *caritas infusa*, but rather is from the outset an ontological possibility of human existence of which man dimly knows. Faith is from the outset an ontological possibility of man that appears in the resolve of despair. It is this that makes it possible for man to understand when he is encountered by the kerygma. For in willing to resolve man wills to believe and to love."[57]

Bultmann's point, in other words, is that unless faith (or "faith working through love") is understood as man's original possibility of authentic historicity, it is impossible to understand human existence outside faith as faith understands it— namely, as "sin." If the possibility of Christian existence is anything other than a possibility which belongs to man *qua* man and for realising which he is therefore responsible from the beginning, he can hardly be held accountable for failing to realise it.

When we consider further Bultmann's statement that demythologisation "is especially demanded by a peculiar contradiction that runs throughout the whole New Testament : . . . man is understood, on the one hand, as a cosmic being and, on the other hand, as an independent self who can win or lose himself in decision,"[58] his meaning is unmistakable. Demythologisation (or existential interpretation) is a "demand of faith itself" because only through it can faith's own insistence on the freedom and transcendence of God and the freedom and responsibility of man be brought to adequate expression.

---

[57] Schubert M. Ogden (ed.), *Existence and Faith: Shorter Writings of Rudolf Bultmann,* New York: Meridian Books, Inc., 1960, p. 108.

[58] *Kerygma und Mythos,* I, p. 23 (pp. 11 f.).

Unless Christian faith is understood as man's original possibility of authentic existence, neither it nor its opposite, nor the God in relation to whom they are the ever-present possibilities for man's decision, can be adequately understood.

It is hardly surprising, then, that Bultmann is so uncompromising in pressing his claim for radical demythologisation and in doing just about everything other than admitting that "there is a non-demythologisable element in Christianity."[59] What is at stake is not merely the continuation in our time of the church's whole programme of evangelisation, but also the adequate expression of the Christian faith itself. The true *Pathos* of Bultmann's undertaking can be understood and accounted for only when this is recognised.

But having said this, we must go on to say that, for all of Bultmann's emphasis on unlimited demythologisation, he is equally insistent that it is because of the event of Jesus of Nazareth *and it alone* that Christian faith or authentic historical existence is factually possible.

It was with this in mind, of course, that the second of the foregoing propositions was formulated. That it is relevant as an expression of the other major facet of Bultmann's thought may be easily confirmed by reflecting that the reason he can distinguish his view from existential philosophy is the very point it expresses. As we have seen in Section 5, he denies that theology and philosophy are identical and justifies his denial by urging that theology has to do with a unique act of God in Jesus of Nazareth. This act, he says, "first makes possible" the authentic existence that, according to the first proposition, philosophy also knows about and even proclaims as man's original possibility.

The difficulty, however, is that not both of these propositions can be true, since when they are taken together they involve a

[59] This is the groundless claim of G. W. Davis, *Existentialism and Theology: An Investigation of the Contribution of Rudolf Bultmann to Theological Thought*, New York: Philosophical Library, 1957, p. 32. Cf. also the parallel claims of Macquarrie, *op. cit.*, p. 174 and Henderson, *op. cit.*, p. 17.

logical self-contradiction. If, as the first proposition affirms, Christian faith is to be interpreted solely in existential terms as man's original possibility of authentic self-understanding, then it demonstrably follows that it must be independent of any particular historical occurrence. On the other hand, if the second proposition is true and Christian faith has a necessary connection with a particular historical event, then clearly it may not be interpreted without remainder as man's original possibility of authentic historicity.

In short, what is involved when these two propositions are affirmed conjointly is the self-contradictory assertion that Christian existence is a historical (*geschichtlich*) possibility open to man as such and yet first *becomes* possible for him because of a particular historical (*historisch*) event.

That Bultmann is not unaware of this difficulty seems evident when he introduces the distinction between a "possibility in principle" and a "possibility in fact." He argues that, although the natural man has the possibility *in principle* of understanding himself authentically, he does not have this possibility *in fact*, since, as he actually exists, he has always lost this possibility and can recover it only in consequence of God's act in Jesus Christ.

But does this distinction accomplish anything more than merely to restate the difficulty? If Christian existence is a possibility belonging to man *qua* man, and so is something for which he is always responsible—and this is clearly what Bultmann wants to affirm when he says it is a "possibility in principle"—then, in this case at least, the distinction between "possibility in principle" and "possibility in fact" is vacuous. On the other hand, if this distinction is not vacuous but has a positive meaning, then the possibility in question is not an original possibility of man as such that he is always obligated to realise. This can be easily demonstrated.

If, as seems self-evident, the only possibilities one may be held accountable for realising (or not realising) are genuine alternatives between which he can actually choose, then to the extent that Christian existence is a possibility for whose realisation man is responsible, it is a genuine option open to his decision. Recognising that Bultmann explicitly holds that to be "in" faith or "outside" it are possibilities for which man has full responsibility, we cannot avoid the conclusion that the distinction between "in principle" and "in fact" is completely empty when applied to Christian existence. Unless such existence is a "possibility in fact" as well as a "possibility in principle," it cannot be a possibility that man is accountable for realising—although this, *ex hypothesi*, is exactly what it is.

The rule here, of course, is the one stated by Kant : *Du kannst, denn du sollst* ; and unless this rule can be shown to be false—and, as we have indicated, it appears to be self-evident—the conclusion just drawn cannot be evaded.

It may be argued conversely that if the distinction between "possibility in principle" and "possibility in fact" is *not* empty, then the possibility to which it refers cannot be one for whose realisation man simply as such is accountable.

Consider an analogy : the possibility of man's encircling the globe by air has always been a "possibility in principle," although only quite recently has it also become a "possibility in fact." To assert, then, that prior to the time when a machine became available to make such a feat possible, men were still responsible for accomplishing it—or even that after that time those who have had no access to such a machine have been similarly responsible—is surely to assert nonsense.

By the same token, however, to argue with Bultmann that Christian existence has become factually possible only because of the event Jesus of Nazareth means that all the men who lived before that event as well as the vast majority who have lived after it were not at all responsible for realising that possibility. For even if it was a "possibility in principle" for them, it was *not* a "possibility in fact" ; and because it was not factually possible as an alternative to be resolved by their own free decision, it can hardly have been a possibility for which, in any meaningful sense, they were responsible.

When Bultmann affirms that authentic historical existence is factually possible *only* as faith in Jesus Christ, he completely frustrates at least one of his motives for insisting that Christian faith is nothing other than authentic self-understanding. If what accounts for his insistence is that he is concerned to do full justice to the New Testament view that man can win or lose himself by his own responsible decisions, this concern is utterly thwarted as soon as he affirms the second proposition. So far from reflecting an understanding of man as genuinely free and responsible, such an affirmation really implies a quasi-Gnostic conception in which man is understood as the helpless and irresponsible victim of fate. Therefore, if Bultmann is bound to affirm that the possibility of Christian existence is contingent on the prior occurrence of the event Jesus of Nazareth, he cannot but pay the price of surrendering all serious talk of man's freedom and responsibility.

This raises the further question whether the other motive behind his demand for demythologisation and existential interpretation is not also undercut by this affirmation. If, as we saw in Section 3, modern man's picture of himself and his world requires the rejection of (1) everything that cannot be affirmed to have happened because it cannot be established in accordance with the general demands of science, and (2) everything that violates the unity of man's selfhood by representing him as at the mercy of powers whose agency is independent of his own responsible decisions—if this is true, then Bultmann completely frustrates his concern to do justice to modern man's situation when he asserts that Christian existence is factually possible only as faith in Jesus Christ. For under what conditions could it be established scientifically (and since it is an "objective" proposition, this is the only way it could be established) that it is only as faith in the Christian kerygma that authentic self-understanding is actually realisable ? Could any other standpoint than that of the One "unto whom all hearts are open, all desires known" conceivably suffice to confirm such an absolute assertion ?

Furthermore, even if, *per impossibile*, such an assertion could be established, what possible relevance could it have for one who knows his existence can be won or lost only by his own responsible decisions ?

No, the only possible answer is that in this respect, also, Bultmann completely stultifies his own express concern. When it is viewed from the standpoint of modern man's picture of himself and his world, his claim that authentic historicity is factually possible only in Jesus Christ must be regarded as just as incredible and irrelevant as the other myths with which it properly belongs.

But if this is true, what could possibly explain Bultmann's making such a claim ? If in making it he not only frustrates his concern to express adequately faith's own understanding of man as free and responsible, but also involves himself in the very mythology he wants to escape, what accounts for his claim ?

It should be obvious that if our answer is to be anything more than an empty speculation or an impertinent prying into Bultmann's religious life, it must be sought in his own statements concerning his motivation. The difficulty, however, is that none of the reasons he himself gives for his claim can really serve to justify it. This is evident from the following considerations.

In the argument examined in Section 5, Bultmann rests his case against existential philosophy on three propositions :

1. Unlike the New Testament (and theology), philosophy assumes that the possibility of genuine historicity is always factually realisable and is, in fact, realised insofar as man chooses to understand himself authentically.

2. Philosophy can make this assumption only because, again unlike the New Testament and theology, it denies that "man

himself is completely and utterly fallen" and therefore understands his fallenness as "a condition that does not extend to his inmost self."[60]

3. If, however, one rejects such an understanding and insists that man *is* completely fallen, one must also deny that authentic existence is always factually realisable and may therefore legitimately claim it can be realised in fact only in Jesus Christ.

If these propositions are carefully examined, it is evident that the conclusion drawn is a *non sequitur*. Contrary to Bultmann's argument, one may very well affirm that "man himself is completely and utterly fallen" (and that the particular philosophers against whom Bultmann is arguing may not affirm this is neither here nor there), and yet at the same time also affirm that the possibility of authentic existence is always factually realisable. The only condition under which this may not be done is that this possibility can be realised in fact only because of a particular historical event; but so far from having been established, this condition is the very thing that has to be proved. In other words, one may not conclude, as Bultmann does, that because man is radically fallen salvation is possible only in Jesus Christ without illicitly assuming the precise point at issue.

By the same token, it is also wrong to assume that because one denies this kind of exclusivism to the event of Jesus Christ he must also necessarily deny that man is radically fallen.[61] It

---

[60] *Kerygma und Mythos*, I, p. 36 (pp. 28 f.).

[61] Buri is completely correct in claiming that Bultmann falsely "generalises distortions that are always possible" when he assumes that the only alternative to his exclusivistic christocentrism is a position that denies the radical character both of man's fallenness and of God's grace (cf. *Kerygma und Mythos*, II, p. 97). Simply because someone may affirm that authentic existence is always realisable on the ground that man is not completely fallen, it does not follow that this is the *only* basis on which this affirmation may be made. One cannot but think that Bultmann's cavalier rejection of the views of Kamlah and Heidegger as involving a radical "wilfulness" rests less on an examination of their claims than on an *a priori* argument that begs the very question at issue.

is at least conceivable that what makes authentic existence everywhere factually possible is not that man is not completely fallen, but that, in spite of his fallenness, he is everlastingly the object of God's love, which is omnipresently efficacious as a redemptive possibility. Nor is it to the point to argue that man's radical fallenness consists precisely in constantly closing himself against this possibility. For even if this is exactly what occurs, the first conclusion to be drawn from it is not that man needs Jesus Christ, but that he needs a new self-understanding in which his fallenness is overcome by laying hold of this possibility of life in God's love. And whether the latter conclusion necessarily implies the former or, on the contrary, is in some sense independent of it is the very question under discussion.

Thus, Bultmann's statement quoted earlier[62] that "Christian faith is faith in Christ because it is faith in the revealed love of God" can be true only if "Jesus Christ" and "the revealed love of God" are merely two ways of saying the same thing. That Bultmann *assumes* this in the context from which the statement is taken can hardly be doubted ; but that he ever *demonstrates* it, even in his extended discussion of "the question of natural revelation,"[63] is an entirely different matter. Indeed, he everywhere begs the question by simply taking for granted the very point that, as he himself admits, has to be proved if faith is to "acquire self-confidence."[64]

Likewise, one must reject the other line of argument that is also quite common in Bultmann's writings. He frequently attempts to show that the only alternative to his affirmation that authentic existence is factually possible solely in Jesus

---

[62] *Kerygma und Mythos*, i, p. 39 (p. 32).

[63] Cf. *Glauben und Verstehen*, Vol. ii, Tübingen: J. C. B. Mohr, 1952, pp. 79-104 (English translation by J. C. G. Greig in Rudolf Bultmann, *Essays, Philosophical and Theological*, London: S.C.M. Press, Ltd., 1955, pp. 90-118). Cf. also *Existence and Faith*, pp. 82 ff.

[64] *Kerygma und Mythos*, i, p. 32 (p. 23).

Christ is a position in which faith is reduced to mere intellectual assent and its object to "timeless truths" or a "world-view." Thus he argues, for example, that

> . . . if *the scandal of Christianity* is that forgiveness is proclaimed in this *one* word of Christ and nowhere else, then faith stands in the constant crisis this scandal evokes : What right does this proclamation have to hold itself to be the only legitimate one ? What right has an ordinary man whom I do not know and who does not know me to promise me the forgiveness of my sin in the name of God merely because he accidentally happens to be entrusted with the preaching office of the church ?

But does this mean anything else than that man struggles against the concrete judgment that is factually spoken to *him* and against him ? That he is indeed willing to accept this judgment as something general, something that he himself can pronounce—that he is indeed willing to acknowledge in general the forgiveness that, in fact, can only be concretely promised to him as an individual person ? And does this mean anything else than that he is indeed willing to acknowledge the *idea* of sin, the *idea* of forgiveness, the *idea* of God, but not God himself ? What Christianity means by *the incarnation of God* is that his reality is not that of an idea, but that of a concrete occurrence ; and that the reality of his forgiveness is only encountered in the concrete word legitimated by him.[65]

Bultmann's assumption, clearly, is that one can acknowledge his own sinfulness and need for God's forgiveness only by

---

[65] *Glauben und Verstehen*, II, pp. 14 f. (p. 16). Bultmann's most recent statements of this same argument, which are equally vulnerable to the same objections, are to be found in his discussion with Karl Jaspers. Cf. *Kerygma und Mythos*, III, pp. 55 f., 57 ff. (English translation in Karl Jaspers and Rudolf Bultmann, *Myth and Christianity*, New York: The Noonday Press, 1958, pp. 66 f., 69 ff.); and on the same point, cf. especially *Glauben und Verstehen*, III, pp. 211 f.

conceding that this forgiveness is proclaimed solely in Jesus Christ. But will this assumption bear scrutiny ? Is it true, for example, that the only condition under which I can honestly admit I am a liar is also to affirm that the way in which I am brought to such an admission is the only way I *could* be brought to it ? Is not rather the very meaning of being a liar, of being one who has more or less consciously suppressed the truth, such that one could *always* have admitted his dishonesty ? Is not the connection between the event of admission itself and the other events that may occur simultaneously with it—say, the judgment of a friend through which I am confronted with my mendacity—purely a connection *de facto* and not *de iure* ?

By analogy, then, is it not false to argue that because the faithful acceptance of God's forgiveness is not simply belief in an idea, but has to be an event of my personal existence, it can take place only through an encounter with the message of the church ? Could I not always have accepted it, with or without such encounter, provided only that I am always confronted by the event of God's forgiveness and so always have the possibility of accepting it ?

The answers to these questions seem obvious. And they confirm the judgment that Bultmann begs the question when he argues that faith in God can be more than a mere "worldview" only as faith in Jesus Christ. Although we may agree that faith must indeed be an event of *existentiell* decision, rather than the intellection of timeless truths, Bultmann completely fails to show that such a requirement has any necessary connection with what he takes to be the distinctive Christian claim. So far as his argument goes, all that is required is *some* event in which God's grace becomes a concrete occurrence and is received by a decision of faith.[66]

---

[66] Our argument here also applies *mutatis mutandis* to the position presented by James M. Robinson in *A New Quest of the Historical Jesus*, London: S.C.M. Press, Ltd., 1959, pp. 80 ff. Like Bultmann, Robinson illicitly argues from an

Significantly, however, the one thing Bultmann's argument does establish (and the same thing may be also said about the other argument considered above) is that *the only meaning the event Jesus Christ has is a purely existential meaning.* Unless this were true, it would be impossible for Bultmann to argue that to refuse to believe in this event is identical with opting for an inauthentic self-understanding. Therefore, what he undoubtedly proves in his abortive attempts to show that authentic existence is factually possible only in Jesus Christ is that the demand to believe in Christ and the demand to understand oneself authentically are one and the same thing.

Thus, ironically enough, even in his efforts to demonstrate the contrary, Bultmann inadvertently shows that Christian existence is *not* a possibility that can be realised solely because of Jesus of Nazareth. For if authentic existence must by its very nature always be a "possibility in fact" as well as a "possibility in principle," to affirm that the entire meaning of faith is to understand oneself authentically is also to affirm that faith is by no means completely contingent on a particular historical event.

Even so, Bultmann's theology, as it now stands, is shot through with an inconsistency that completely determines its basic structure and movement. Although none of the reasons he adduces justify his claim that authentic historicity is factually possible only in Jesus Christ, he undoubtedly makes this

---

inexhaustive dichotomy when he juxtaposes "principle" and "history" (or "truth" and "event") and regards the second term as necessarily referring to the particular occurrence Jesus of Nazareth. Consequently, his polemic against the view represented by Buri and ourselves (in "Bultmann's Project of Demythologisation and the Problem of Theology and Philosophy," *Journal of Religion*, July, 1957, pp. 156-173) is completely lacking in force. The real alternative to a mythological particularism, which makes everything turn on the *human events* of Jesus and the proclamation of the church, is not to conceive the kerygma as "the objectivation of a truth" or "a symbolised principle," but to present it as the historical articulation of the *divine event* of grace and judgment.

claim and, moreover, intends it in a sense quite incompatible with the other major facet of his thought. It cannot be argued that this claim is simply an exaggerated and therefore unfortunate way of saying something very different from what it appears to say. Whatever his motives, Bultmann undoubtedly makes the claim and intends it to be understood for exactly what it seems to be.

By doing so, however—or, more accurately, by doing so conjointly with asserting that demythologisation is unqualifiedly necessary (or that Christian faith is to be interpreted solely in existential terms)—he completely nullifies his own constructive proposal for a solution to the contemporary theological problem. For the first as well as the last demand of all serious thought is that it be internally consistent ; and this, Bultmann's proposal most certainly is not.

Therefore, the first thing to do in moving towards a tenable solution is to reject the way in which Bultmann proposes to solve the problem. This does not mean that his proposal is completely without value. On the contrary, as we affirmed in Chapter I, an inconsistent theology may still be immensely significant as a resource for constructive reflection. That this is pre-eminently true in the case of Bultmann has long since become clear. He has not only provided the principal resources for arriving at what *is* a tenable solution, but has also performed the invaluable service of focusing the central problem and thereby constraining the rest of us to labour to solve it. To attempt to understand his thought and to come to terms with it critically is to be literally forced to a decision as to how the theological problem of our time can be solved.

In this respect, we may well say of Bultmann what Wilhelm Pauck once said of Karl Barth in a truly prophetic analysis of Barth's early thought : "[He] is not *the* prophet of the new Christianity. He is the 'preacher in the wilderness.' His voice rings in our ears, and we will not forget his message, but we must wait for another."[67]

Who this "other" will be—or, better, what the "message" will be that he will certainly proclaim—is the subject of our concluding chapter.

---

[67] *Karl Barth, Prophet of a New Christianity?* New York: Harper & Brothers, 1931, p. 220. The implied resemblance of Bultmann to the "early" Barth is not unintended. Indeed, as the epigraph to this study should suggest, the position of Barth in *Der Römerbrief* is much more radical than Bultmann's in being free of any mythological claims for a unique revelation in Jesus Christ. To be sure, this point has seldom been appreciated both because of the "neo-orthodoxy" of Barth's later development and the misleading impression created by Edwyn C. Hoskyns's translation of *The Epistle to the Romans*, London: Oxford University Press, 1933. Furthermore, as Pauck showed with great insight, there was a certain instability even in Barth's early position, which in part explains the unfortunate direction of his subsequent work. Nevertheless, there can be no question that what has now been proposed by Bultmann as a generalised solution to the contemporary theological problem stands in the strictest continuity with the original "dialectical theology." Moreover, there are insights in Barth's earlier work (especially *Der Römerbrief* Munich: Christian Kaiser Verlag, 2nd ed., 1922; *Die Auferstehung der Toten,* Munich: Christian Kaiser Verlag, 2nd ed., 1925; and *Das Wort Gottes und die Theologie,* Munich: Christian Kaiser Verlag, 2nd ed, 1925) which point beyond Bultmann's inconsistency—and Barth's own present *Mythengläubigkeit*! —to a genuine solution of our theological problem. Cf. further the discussion in "The Debate on 'Demythologising,' " *Journal of Bible and Religion,* January, 1959, pp. 17-27, and *Existence and Faith,* pp. 13 ff.

CHAPTER IV

The Outlines of
a Constructive Alternative

9.   THE APPARENT ALTERNATIVES

We come now to the final task of our study. Having attempted first, an integral understanding of Bultmann's proposal and, second, an immanent criticism that was negative in its results, we must now ask how a genuinely tenable alternative to his position is to be achieved.

In order to do this, it is necessary to abandon the immanent standpoint that has been determinative for the discussions of the preceding two chapters. We must now adopt a perspective that in part transcends Bultmann's position and, from that vantage point, attempt to speak to the problem he has sought to solve. Only so can the deadlock presented by his proposal be broken and the possibility realised of achieving a defensible solution to the contemporary problem.

The first principle of such a solution is that *the demand for demythologisation that arises with necessity from the situation of modern man must be accepted without condition.*

That the assumption of this principle is not gratuitous, but fully warranted, seems to us to have been demonstrated by Bultmann and to require little additional confirmation. It should be sufficient simply to recall the argument analysed in Section 3 to convince oneself that this must be the presupposition of any responsible contemporary theology. Bultmann has conclusively shown that to try to continue a mode of thought that has long since been called in question and has therefore become increasingly incredible and irrelevant to the modern cultural consciousness is to attempt something doomed before it is even begun. If the content of faith is to be presented today in a form that can be "understanded of the people"—and this, it must not be forgotten, is one of the goals of the perennial theological task—there is no other choice but to abandon completely a mythological manner of representation.

This does not mean that mythological language as such can no longer be used in theology and preaching. The absurd notion that demythologisation entails the expurgation of all mythological concepts completely misrepresents Bultmann's intention. His point is not that mythology may not be used, but that it may no longer be regarded as the only or even the most appropriate conceptuality for expressing Christian kerygma. When we say that a mythological mode of thought must be completely abandoned, we mean it must be abandoned as the sole or proper means for presenting the Christian understanding of existence. Mythological concepts may by all means still be used, but they can be used responsibly only as "symbols" or "ciphers," that is, only if they are also constantly *interpreted* in nonmythological (or existential) terms.

The statement is often made when Bultmann argues in this way, he "over-estimates the intellectual stumbling-block which myth is supposed to put in the way of accepting the Christian faith."[1] But this statement is completely unconvincing. If Bultmann's own definition of myth is strictly adhered to (and it is interesting that this is almost never done by those who make such pronouncements), the evidence is overwhelming that he does not at all exaggerate the extent to which the mythological concepts of traditional theology have become

---

[1] John Macquarrie, *An Existentialist Theology: A Comparison of Heidegger and Bultmann*, London: S.C.M. Press, Ltd., 1955, p. 246.

incredible and irrelevant. Nor is it necessary to look for such evidence in the great urban centres of our culture that are admittedly almost entirely secularised and so profoundly estranged from the conventional forms in which the gospel has been communicated. On the contrary, even in the heart of "the Bible belt" itself, as can be attested by any one who is called to work there, the industrial and technological revolutions have long been under way, together with the corresponding changes in man's picture of himself and his world.

In fact, it is in just such a situation that the profundity of Bultmann's argument is disclosed. Although the theological forms of the past continue to exist in a way they do not in a more secularised situation, the striking thing is the rapidity with which they are being reduced to a marginal existence. This is especially in evidence among the present generation of the suburban middle class. Time and again in counselling and teaching, one encounters members of this group whose attempts to bring into some kind of unity the insubstantial mythologies of their "fundamentalist" heritage and the stubborn reality of the modern world are only too painfully obvious.

The same thing is also evidenced by the extreme " culture-Protestantism" so often observed to characterise the preaching and teaching of the American churches. In the absence of a truly adequate conceptuality in which the gospel can be expressed, the unavoidable need to demythologise it makes use of whatever resources are at hand—and this usually means one or another of the various forms of "folk religion" current in the situation.[2] This is not to say that the *only* explanation of the present infatuation with Norman Vincent Peale's "cult of reassurance" or the other types of a purely cultural Christianity is the ever-present need for a demythologised gospel. But it is to say that this need is far more important

---

[2] For a discussion of the concept of "folk religion" see A. Roy Eckardt, *The Surge of Piety in America*, New York: Association Press, 1958, pp. 42 ff.

for such infatuation than most of the pundits seem to have suspected.

However, even if the latent demand for demythologisation is not nearly as widespread as we are claiming, at least among the cultured elements of the population there tends to be an almost complete indifference to the church and its traditional message of sin and grace. To be sure, when this is pointed out, a common response among certain churchmen is to fulminate about "the little flock" and "the great crowd" and to take solace from Paul's castigation of the "wisdom of the wise" in the opening chapter of First Corinthians. But can we any longer afford the luxury of such smug indignation? Can the church risk assuming that the "folly" of men is as dear to God as their "wisdom," or, as is also commonly implied, that "the foolishness of God" and "the foolishness of men" are simply two ways of talking about the same thing? Can we continue to alienate precisely those whose gifts we so desperately need and apart from whose co-operation our mission in the world must become increasingly precarious?

There is an ancient and venerable tradition in the church (which derives, however, from the heritage of the Greeks rather than from the Bible) that God is completely independent of his creation and so has no need of men for accomplishing his work in the world. By analogy, the church also has been regarded as entirely independent of the "world" in the sense of requiring nothing from it in order to be the church. But, as Scripture everywhere reminds us, God *does* have need of his creatures, and the church, *a fortiori*, can ill afford to do without the talents with which the world, by God's providence, presents it.

And yet this is exactly the risk we run when we assume, as we too often do, that we can continue to preach the gospel in a form that makes it seem incredible and irrelevant to cultured men. Until we translate this gospel into a language that enlightened men to-day can understand, we are depriving ourselves of the very resources on which the continued success of our witness most certainly depends.

In arguing in this way, we are obviously taking for granted that a demythologised restatement of the kerygma can be achieved ; and that we firmly believe this will presently become evident when we set forth reasons to justify such a conviction. But the main point here is that even if such a restatement were *not* possible, the demand to demythologise the kerygma would still be unavoidable.

This is what we mean when we say this demand must be accepted without condition. If to be a Christian means to say yes where I otherwise say no, or where I do not have the right to say anything at all, then my only choice is to refuse to be a Christian. Expressed differently : if the price for becoming a faithful follower of Jesus Christ is some form of self-destruction, whether of the body or of the mind—*sacrificium corporis*, *sacrificium intellectus*—then there is no alternative but that the price remain unpaid.

This must be stressed because it is absolutely essential to the argument of this concluding chapter. Modern man, as Dietrich Bonhoeffer has told us, has "come of age"[3] ; and though this process by no means represents an unambiguous gain and is, in fact, marked by the estrangement from the depths that seems to be the cost of human maturation, it is still a positive step forward ; and those of us who so richly benefit from it should be the last to despise it. In any event, it is an irreversible step, and if we are at all honest with ourselves we will know we have no other alternative than to live in the world in which God has seen fit to place us.

---

[3] Cf. *Letters and Papers from Prison*, trans. by R. H. Fuller, London: S.C.M. Press, 1953, pp. 122 ff. Cf. also Ronald Gregor Smith, *The New Man: Christianity and Man's Coming of Age*, New York: Harper & Brothers, 1956, where Bonhoeffer's insight is independently developed in the context of a discussion also with Bultmann. It is significant that Smith's position apparently departs from Bultmann's at the very point at which the present study also finds it impossible to go with it (cf., e.g., p. 91).

To say this, of course, is to take up a position on one side of a controversy going on now for some two hundred years, or, at any rate, since the beginning of the distinctly modern period in theological thought. We have aligned ourselves with that "liberal" tradition in Protestant Christianity that counts among the great names in its history those of Schleiermacher, Ritschl, Herrmann, Harnack, and Troeltsch, and more recently, Schweitzer and the early Barth and, in part at least, Bultmann. It is to this same tradition that most of the creative figures in the last century and a half of American theology also belong. For we must number here not only the names of Bushnell, Clarke, and Rauschenbusch, not to mention those of "the Chicago School" and Macintosh, but those of the brothers Niebuhr and (if America may claim him!) Tillich as well.[4] Finally, we may also mention the several members of the self-consciously "neo-liberal" movement that developed at the University of Chicago and is heavily indebted philosophically to the creative work of Alfred North Whitehead.[5]

[4] Any doubts whether Reinhold Niebuhr belongs in this tradition have surely been dispelled by his more recent writings. His forthright statements in connection with the heresy trials some years ago in the North-west Synod of the United Lutheran Church made his position crystal clear (cf. *Christianity and Crisis*, December 26, 1955, pp. 171 f. and especially February 6, 1956, pp. 6 f.). Most recently, in his contribution to the *Christian Century*'s series, "How My Mind Has Changed," he affirms, in face of what he considers reactionary tendencies in contemporary theology, that he "is a liberal at heart, and that many of [his] broadsides against liberalism were indiscriminate" (May 11, 1960, p. 568). Equally impressive is H. Richard Niebuhr's article in the same series. Like his brother, he sees the developments currently inspired by Karl Barth as dangerously reactionary and argues that the better course for contemporary theology is to resume "the general line of march represented by the evangelical, empirical, and critical movement" of the modern period. Niebuhr also acknowledges what some of us have long suspected, that among contemporary theologians it is Bultmann "above all" with whom he feels "great kinship . . . in his intentions" (March 2, 1960, p. 250). Likewise, all the writings of Paul Tillich give evidence of the authentic liberal's concern. This is especially true of his *Systematic Theology*, which, as becomes increasingly evident, may be fairly characterised as a twentieth-century restatement of the basic position of Schleiermacher's *Glaubenslehre*.

[5] The leading figures here are Henry Nelson Wieman and, on the more philosophical side, Charles Hartshorne. Cf. also James Luther Adams, *Taking*

What makes this long and diverse tradition essentially *one* is that those who have belonged to it have been profoundly in earnest about being modern men in a distinctly modern world. Although they have also been concerned to stand squarely within the tradition of the apostolic church, they have exhibited no willingness whatever to sacrifice their modernity to their Christianity. They have insisted, rather, on living fully and completely within modern culture and, so far from considering this treason to God, have looked upon it as the only way they could be faithful to him.

When we say, then, that to-day, in our situation, the demand for demythologisation must be accepted without condition, we are simply saying that at least this much of the liberal tradition is an enduring achievement. However much we may have to criticise liberal theology's constructive formulations, the theology we ourselves must strive to formulate can only go *beyond* liberalism, not *behind* it.

In affirming this we have already taken the decisive step in breaking the deadlock into which Bultmann's attempt to formulate such a theology has led. For we have said, in effect, that of the two alternatives to his position variously represented by the other participants in the demythologising discussion, only one is really an alternative. If the demand for demythologisation is unavoidable and so must be accepted by theology unconditionally, the position of the "right" is clearly untenable. Whereas Bultmann's "centre" position is structurally inconsistent and is therefore indefensible on formal grounds alone, the general position of the "right," as represented, say, by Karl Barth, involves the rejection or at least

Time Seriously, Glencoe, Illinois: The Free Press, 1957; Bernard M. Loomer, "Christian Faith and Process Philosophy," *Journal of Religion*, July, 1949, pp. 181-203; Bernard Eugene Meland, *Faith and Culture*, New York: Oxford University Press, 1953; Wilhelm Pauck, *The Heritage of the Reformation*, Glencoe, Illinois: The Free Press, 1950; and Daniel Day Williams, *God's Grace and Man's Hope*, New York: Harper & Brothers, 1949.

qualification of the demand for demythologisation and so is invalidated on the material grounds we have just considered.

It follows, then, provided the possibilities have been exhausted, that the only *real* alternative is the general viewpoint of the "left," which has been represented on the Continent by Fritz Buri and, to some extent, is found in much that is significant in American and English theology.[6]

In order to make the implications of our position as clear as possible, we may develop this argument at greater length.

We may show, first, that there cannot possibly be an alternative other than the three typically represented by Bultmann, Barth, and Buri. To do this, it is sufficient to point out that if the principle in terms of which alternatives are to be conceived is such as to exclude more than two, then the question of a "third" possibility is a meaningless question. Thus, if

[6] For example, Reinhold Niebuhr's important but seldom appreciated doctrine of the "hidden Christ" (cf. *The Nature and Destiny of Man*, Vol. II, New York: Charles Scribner's Sons, 1943, pp. 109 f., n. 6), as well as the whole character of his unmistakably "empirical" theology reflects such a position. The same thing is true of the writings of H. Richard Niebuhr, who has been outspokenly critical of an idolatrous "Christism" in the name of "radical monotheism" (cf., e.g., *The Purpose of the Church and Its Ministry*, New York: Harper & Brothers, 1956, pp. 44 ff.). Indeed, Niebuhr has recently provided an eloquent statement bearing on the very point at issue in this study. "So far as I could see and can now see," he writes, "that miracle [*sic* of faith] has been wrought among us by and through Jesus Christ. I do not have the evidence which allows me to say that the miracle of faith in God is worked only by Jesus Christ and that it is never given to men outside the sphere of his working, though I may say that where I note its presence I posit the presence also of something like Jesus Christ" (cf. *Christian Century*, March 2, 1960, p. 249). Similarly, Tillich has long been on record as rejecting an exclusivistic christocentrism, though such rejection is particularly in evidence in the whole last portion of his *Systematic Theology*, Vol. II, Chicago: The University of Chicago Press, 1957. A last example is the Scottish theologian, John Baillie, who for over a generation has provided a much-needed corrective to "the unitarianism of the second person" that is the bane of so much Protestant theology (cf. especially *The Place of Jesus Christ in Modern Christianity*, New York: Charles Scribner's Sons, 1930, pp. 202-212; and *Our Knowledge of God*, New York: Charles Scribner's Sons, 2nd ed., 1959, pp. 17 ff.). In sum, the general position of the "left," with more or less consistency and self-consciousness, is shared by several English-speaking theologians whose origins in liberal theology have never been forgotten or lightly cast aside.

what is at issue is whether "All S is P," it is indifferent whether "Some S is not P" or "No S is P," since in either case the judgment in question is false. Hence, if what is in question is whether in a given theology myth is or is not completely rejected, it is unimportant whether only a little bit of myth or a considerable quantity is accepted; for, in either event, the first possibility is excluded. Therefore, the only conceivable alternatives are those represented, on the one hand, by the two at least apparently self-consistent but mutually exclusive positions of Buri and Barth and, on the other hand, by the third but really pseudo position (analogous to a round square) of Bultmann.

A second point requires more extended comment. It will be recalled from the discussion in Section 7 that the position of the "right," as represented by Barth, rests on the following thesis: The only tenable alternative to Bultmann's position is a theology that (1) rejects or at least qualifies his unconditioned demand for demythologisation and existential interpretation; (2) accepts instead a special biblical hermeneutics or method of interpretation; and (3) in so doing, frees itself to give appropriate emphasis to the event Jesus Christ by means of statements that, from Bultmann's point of view, are mythological. When we say, then, that the position of the "right" is untenable, we mean that to the extent it is simply the claim that what is obviously mythology is to be accepted merely because it is in the New Testament, it cannot be defended for the same reasons any similar claim is indefensible.

This is the point classically made by Bultmann himself in his brief but conclusive reply to Barth's criticism of his demand for demythologisation. "In what sense," he asks, "does Barth appeal to a command for honesty of another or higher type than the command that requires me to hold nothing as true that contradicts the truths which are the factual presupposition of the understanding of the world that guides everything I do ?"[7] This question implies an unanswerable criticism. It makes clear that the only way the position of the "right" can be maintained is by some form of special pleading. That this is actually the case can be documented again and again from the way the defenders of this position typically argue their case.

Consider, for example, the constructive argument presented by John Macquarrie in the concluding sections of his analysis of Bultmann's thought. He argues, very much as Barth, Buri, and we have argued, that Bultmann's position is "inconsistent" because Bultmann "puts forward a view of theology which calls for radical demythologising, and the translation of all transcendent statements into statements about the understanding of the self" and "yet at the same time . . . believes that God has acted decisively in Christ."[8] Since Macquarrie holds that such a belief must be maintained at all costs and that it is endangered by Bultmann's contradictory demand for demythologisation, he concludes the "danger can only be guarded against by the frank acknowledgment that theology is concerned not only with statements about human existence but with statements about God and his activity as well."[9]

It becomes evident, however, that the only way Macquarrie can establish such statements about God's activity is by completely fallacious arguments. Thus, in attempting to prove the objective historicity of the resurrection, he writes : "The question is to be decided not on general grounds of probability —for, after all, we remember that these were unique events in which God was at work—but on the historical evidence available."[10] Not only is it impossible to oppose "general grounds of probability" and "available historical evidence" (as though any "evidence" could have force except by being confirmed as probable on precisely such grounds !), it is also

[7] *Glauben und Verstehen*, Vol. II, Tübingen: J. C. B. Mohr, 1952, p. 235 (English translation by J. C. G. Greig in Rudolf Bultmann, *Essays, Philosophical and Theological*, London: S.C.M. Press, Ltd., 1955, p. 261).
[8] *Op. cit.*, p. 243.   [9] *Ibid.*, pp. 243 f.   [10] *Ibid.*, p. 187.

illicit to beg the very question at issue by appealing to God's alleged activity.

The general line of thought, of which Macquarrie's argument is but an illustration, is thoroughly characteristic of those who defend the alternative of the "right." In one form or another and with individual differences of nuance and emphasis, the same specious argument *a posse ad esse* and the same *petitio principii* repeatedly occur in the various attempts to break the Bultmannian deadlock by rejecting or qualifying the demand for demythologisation. Nor could one expect it to be otherwise. For, in the nature of the case, the only way one can conceivably establish such mythical events as the virgin birth or the resurrection as objective historical events is by illicitly assuming that because they are possible they are also actual (as Karl Barth has rightly been accused of doing[11]) or by simply begging the question and smuggling a presumption as to their historicity into the premises of the demonstration (as is done by Macquarrie).[12] In both cases, logic is sacrificed to some special interest by the adoption of a mode of argument any unbiased mind would regard as indefensible.[13]

But the position of the "right" is untenable for another reason than its special pleading on behalf of incredible assertions. The mythology it supposes it must affirm is completely irrelevant to the real meaning of human existence. If the fulfilment of our lives as persons is dependent on our individual decisions concerning self-understanding, and so is something for which we ourselves are each responsible, then "events" like Jesus' virginal conception, his physical resurrection, his

[11] Cf. the criticism by Christian Hartlich and Walter Sachs in H. W. Bartsch (ed.), *Kerygma und Mythos*, Vol. II, Hamburg: Herbert Reich-Evangelischer Verlag, 1952, pp. 117-121.

[12] Cf. also the almost classic instance of *petitio principii* in the argument for the "fundamental miracles" in Arthur F. Smethurst, *Modern Science and Christian Beliefs*, New York: Abingdon Press, 1955, pp. 215-226.

[13] For an imaginative treatment of the basic point here, see Van A. Harvey, "On Believing What Is Difficult to Understand: A Dialogue," *Journal of Religion*, October, 1959, pp. 219-231.

bodily ascension, and his visible coming again on the clouds of heaven are of no relevance whatever to such fulfilment. Or, to speak more accurately, they are no more relevant (or irrelevant) than any other event of the same basic type.

Thus, if, *per impossibile*, the corpse of a man was actually resuscitated, this would be just as relevant to my salvation as an existing self or person as that the carpenter next door just drove a nail in a two-by-four, or that American technicians have at last been successful in recovering a nose cone that had first been placed in orbit around the earth.

The premise of this conclusion, to repeat, is that man is a genuinely free and responsible being, and therefore his salvation is something that, *coram deo*, he himself has to decide by his understanding of his existence. If this premise is true —and unless it is, it is arguable that "salvation" and all it implies must be meaningless to the modern man—then the second reason the position of the "right" is untenable should be evident.

We must be clear, however, as to what is and is not being said about this position. We are *not* saying it is in every respect an incredible and irrelevant point of view. On the contrary, all we are concerned to claim is that to the extent to which it insists that the Christian message is intrinsically "mythological" in Bultmann's sense of the word, it cannot be defended because it is unacceptable from the standpoint of modern man's picture of himself and his world.

This obviously leaves open the possibility that, at least in some respects, theologies of this general type are still able to speak understandably and relevantly to the contemporary situation. And this unquestionably happens. Indeed, one must say that the tendency of this kind of position is not so much simply to reject the demand for demythologisation as to try in some way to qualify it. Whereas for Bultmann, Buri, and us, the demand for demythologisation is unconditional, for our critics on the "right," it is acceptable, if at all, only under certain conditions. This explains, of course, why within the camp of the "right" itself there is a variety of views lying all the way between a position that seems quite close to Bultmann's (for example, Macquarrie's or Emil Brunner's[14]) and another virtually antithetical to it (for example, that of the Lutheran theologians Ernst Kinder and Walter Künneth or of most of the Roman Catholics).

It also explains why in practically all the representatives of his viewpoint, one repeatedly meets, as a kind of distinguishing refrain, the phrase "not only . . . but also." Thus, in the statement of Macquarrie's quoted above, it is said that "theology is concerned *not only* with statements about human existence, *but* with statements about God and his activity *as well*."[15] The implication is that the reality of God and his saving act is essentially independent of man and his possibilities of existence, so that it is possible to speak of the one without at the same time speaking of the other. Our position, by contrast, is that a theology is "mythological," and so untenable, to the extent to which it denies that statements about God may be interpreted as statements about man. By this we mean *not* that theology may not speak directly about "God and his activity," but simply that whenever it does so speak, its statements must be at least implicitly about man and his possibilities of self-understanding if they are not to be incredible and irrelevant. In *this* sense, "statements about God and his activity" *are* "statements about human existence," and *vice versa*.

The question, however, is whether such a position is not also untenable as a solution to the theological problem, although, naturally, for a very different reason. Granted that Buri, say, is quite prepared to take this position and so is beyond reproach in accepting the demand for demythologisation without con-

[14] Cf. especially Brunner's *Wahrheit als Begegnung*, Zürich: Zwingli Verlag, 1938, which anticipates much of Bultmann's constructive argument in "Neues Testament und Mythologie."

[15] *Op. cit.*, pp. 243 f.; italics added.

dition, can he do this except by surrendering the very basis of the whole theological enterprise ? Is not the fact that his criticism of Bultmann culminates in a demand for "dekerygmatisation" sufficient warning that his solution, too, is finally indefensible ?

This question sets the third task for the present section of our discussion. We must show how this sole remaining alternative actually does provide a tenable solution to the theological problem.

To do this, we must remind ourselves of the other pole of this problem and so make clear we are *not* saying that simply because a theology completely rids itself of an outworn mythological conceptuality it is *ipso facto* an adequate Christian theology. On the contrary, there is a second principle that must also be accepted without condition by any responsible attempt at theological formulation. This is the principle that *the sole norm of every legitimate theological assertion is the revealed word of God declared in Jesus Christ, expressed in Holy Scripture, and made concretely present in the proclamation of the church through its word and sacraments.*

We stated above that one of the goals of the perennial theological task is to express this revealed word of God or kerygma in a conceptuality understandable to those to whom it is addressed ; and the burden of our argument to this point has been to show that in our particular situation this requires an unconditional acceptance of the demand for demythologisation. Our point now, however, is that the other goal of Christian theology must be to express as appropriately as possible *just this particular gospel* and not any other word that may have been uttered in the course of human history. Therefore, the second criterion for measuring the adequacy of theological work is the extent to which it gives expression to the *fides quæ creditur* by and for which the church is called into being.

This does not imply that one may simply take for granted

that the formulation of a theology in this sense is still a live possibility in the distinctively modern situation. On the contrary, we have tried to make clear that theology can continue to be a relevant undertaking only insofar as the kerygma can be consistently demythologised. But even if this were impossible and the kerygma were incapable of demythologisation, the second norm of theological restatement would still be the gospel that is the sole source and object of authentic Christian faith. Theology to-day may indeed have become impossible, but if it is still to be theology in any meaningful sense, this can only be because its self-acknowledged task is one and the same with the perennial theological task of the Christian community.

The question we must answer, then, is whether the position of the "left," which, if our argument is correct, is the only alternative still open to us, can be regarded as tenable from the standpoint of this second theological principle. This does not mean that we also have to consider whether the particular formulation of this position by Fritz Buri is in all respects acceptable when judged by this principle. Much less does it mean that we have any concern whatever to defend the relevance and legitimacy of Buri's demand for "dekerygmatisation." Aside from the fact that Buri himself has subsequently had second thoughts about this demand,[16] our sole concern here, just as in our earlier examination of the position of the "right," is to show the extent to which the position of the "left" as such is adequate when judged by the relevant theological principle. The only thing we are interested in establishing is whether consistent demythologisation (or existential interpretation) is

[16] Cf., e.g., the Epilogue to his small book of homilies, *Das lebendige Wort*, Hamburg: Herbert Reich-Evangelischer Verlag, 1957; and the Preface to the first volume of his *Dogmatik als Selbstverständnis des christlichen Glaubens*, Bern: Paul Haupt Verlag, 1956. Other more recent writings as well make clear that Buri now recognises that what is required is not dekerygmatisation (except in some inadequate sense of the word "kerygma"), but rather an existential restatement that will permit the kerygma really to come into its own. Cf., e.g., *Weg des Glaubens*, Munich: Ernst Reinhardt Verlag, 1958.

at least permitted, if not demanded, by the revealed word of God.

We also will do well to remember, however, that, by its very nature, every attempt to answer this question must finally presuppose itself. To answer it, we must establish, first of all, what this revealed word of God is; and yet to do this is obviously impossible except by employing the very method thereby to be justified. In other words, we cannot escape the fact that all theological argument, like all philosophical argument, is circular. As Whitehead remarks, "the sole appeal is to intuition"; and this means, among other things, that the method of a theology and its content are mutually interdependent.[17]

In order to show that the position of the "left" is defensible from the standpoint of what the kerygma itself permits or requires, we can do nothing but appeal to an understanding of this message with which such a position is already inseparably bound. All exegesis, as Bultmann has so often reminded us, necessarily takes place within a circle;[18] and short of the desperate expedient of appealing to some *ex cathedra* pronouncement to settle our theological differences, we have no alternative but to continue to share with one another in a spirit of openness to mutual criticism whatever understanding of his truth God has so far been pleased to give us.

With these cautions in mind, we may attempt to answer our central question. We may begin by recalling that the implication of the position of the "left," or of consistent demythologisation and existential interpretation, is that Christian existence is always a "possibility in fact" as well as a "possibility in principle." This may also be expressed by saying that the specific possibility of faith in Jesus Christ is

[17] Cf. Paul Tillich, *Systematic Theology*, Vol. I, Chicago: The University of Chicago Press, 1951, pp. 11 and 58.

[18] Cf., for a quite recent statement, *Glauben und Verstehen*, Vol. III, Tübingen: J. C. B. Mohr, 1960, pp. 178 ff.

one and the same with a general ontological possibility belonging to man simply as such.

The difficulty with the second statement is that it may mistakenly suggest that the possibility in question literally "belongs" to man, in the sense of something he possesses independently of his relationship with God, and so is able to dispose of as and when he pleases. The truth is that this possibility is not man's own inalienable possession, but rather is constantly *being made possible for him* by virtue of his inescapable relation to the ultimate source of his existence. To be human means to stand *coram deo* and, by reason of such standing, to be continually confronted with the gift and demand of authentic human existence.

It is in this, and in this sense alone, that the implication of consistent demythologisation has to be understood. All that is necessary to set forth this alternative to the untenable positions of the "right" and the "centre" is the acknowledgment that the possibility of Christian existence is an original possibility of man before God.

In other words, all that is required of one who would take seriously the demand for demythologisation and existential interpretation is that he take with equal seriousness the freedom and transcendence of God and the freedom and responsibility of man. To affirm that all "statements about God and his activity" may be interpreted without remainder as "statements about human existence" need mean nothing more than that one is prepared to accept without condition that the redemptive grace of God is always given to us and to all men in every situation of our lives, and therefore the authentic existence in faith and love it continually makes possible is something for which each of us is primordially responsible.

This means that the real question we have to answer is whether the revealed word of God or kerygma permits this kind of radical emphasis on the freedom of God and the freedom of man. As soon as the question is put in this way, however, we confess it scarcely seems to require an answer. If anything can be said with certainty about the Christian kerygma, it is that it not only permits but absolutely requires just this kind of emphasis and, indeed, its inmost meaning is simply the decisive manifestation of this same double freedom. In fact, we must say with Emil Brunner that the very "content of Holy Scripture" is this "relationship of personal correspondence" in which the freedom of God and the freedom of man are taken with complete seriousness.[19]

There are several ways in which this could be documented exegetically, although all we can do here is to present three separate lines of evidence that seem to converge on this one affirmation.

In the first place, the New Testament never doubts for an instant that before God each individual person is entirely and radically responsible for his final destiny. However much it may make use of conceptualities, such as Gnosticism, in which this radical responsibility can hardly be expressed, its own essential spirit and concern clearly point in a different direction. The classic proof of this is Paul's affirmation in Romans 1 : 20 f. : "So they are without excuse ; for although they knew God they did not honour him as God or give thanks to him, but they became futile in their thinking and their senseless minds were darkened." Unlike many a Protestant exegete whose sound aversion against a Catholic *theologia naturalis* has not carried him as far away from that position as he may have supposed, Paul does not say that the original revelation of God in "the things that have been made" discloses merely the "concept of God" or the "question concerning God" or a purely "negative knowledge" or, at any rate, something less than a full and perfect knowledge of him.[20] On the contrary

[19] Cf. Emil Brunner, *op. cit.*, pp. 49 and 35 (English translation by A. W. Loos in Emil Brunner, *The Divine-Human Encounter*, Philadelphia: The Westminster Press, 1943, pp. 66 and 48).

[20] All the quoted phrases are from Bultmann's discussion of "the question of natural revelation," *Glauben und Verstehen*, II, pp. 79-104 (pp. 90-118), and

he affirms simply that "what can be known about God is plain to them, because God has shown it to them" and so leaves no doubt that the content of this primordial revelation is precisely identical with the "new" knowledge now to be laid hold of in the "obedience of faith."

In other words, Paul's conviction, like that of Scripture as a whole, is that men are utterly and radically responsible because God has always made himself known to them as gracious Father and has thereby deprived them of all excuse for their self-willed estrangement from his holy presence.

In the second place, the only basis of man's salvation the New Testament knows anything about is the everlasting love of God that is primordially active in the mighty works of creation, preservation, and redemption. Here again we may appeal to Paul, who, in the course of his argument in the fifteenth chapter of First Corinthians, makes the following significant statements: "Then comes the end when [Christ] delivers the kingdom to God the father after destroying every rule and every authority and power. For he must reign until he has put all his enemies under his feet. The last enemy to be destroyed is death. 'For God has put all things in subjection under his feet.' But when it says, 'All things are put in subjection under him,' it is plain that he is excepted who put all things under him. When all things are subjected to him, then the Son himself will also be subjected to him who put all things under him, that God may be everything to every one" (vv. 24-28).

---

are thoroughly typical of his way of dealing with this question. Luther himself seems to have been responsible for this kind of quasi-Catholic understanding of "natural revelation" in Protestant theology. At any rate, according to the evidence presented by P. S. Watson, *Let God Be God*, London: The Epworth Press, 1947, pp. 76 ff., he was constantly torn between affirming with Paul that men are "without excuse" (and all this implies, including "a possibility of salvation for men who have never actually heard of Christ" [p. 93]) and affirming that all that is revealed in "natural revelation" is "the God of power and of law" and not "the God of grace" (pp. 81 ff.).

Whatever else is struggling for expression through this welter of mythological images, one thing is surely being affirmed : The peculiarly Christian economy of salvation has a definitely subordinate role in the ultimate outworking of God's purposes. Like the other New Testament witnesses Paul takes for granted that God and God alone is the final source of authentic human life.

To affirm, as is so often done, particularly by Protestant theologians, that the faith of the New Testament is "christocentric" is significantly to alter the New Testament's own express emphasis. From its standpoint, the assertion that faith is "christocentric" is at best an elliptical assertion and, like other such assertions, constantly susceptible to misunderstanding and distortion. Unless it is made clear not only that "we are Christ's," but that "Christ is God's" (I Cor. 3 : 23 ; cf. 11 : 3), that is, unless the *theocentric* basis and sanction of "christocentrism" is explicitly acknowledged, emphasis on Jesus Christ can be a snare and a delusion and a mere travesty of authentic apostolic faith. Contrary to Bultmann, who, significantly, offers no scriptural support for his claim, the New Testament does *not* affirm that in Christ our salvation "becomes possible." It affirms, rather, that in him what has always been possible now "becomes manifest," in the sense of being decisively presented in a human word of witness. Its message is not that God "is the one who must be reconciled," which, as Tillich has rightly argued, is the unavoidable implication of the first affirmation, but that "God, who is eternally reconciled, wants us to be reconciled to him."[21]

Therefore, we repeat that the *only* ground of salvation the New Testament knows anything about is the primordial love of God, which is indeed decisively revealed in Jesus the Christ, but is by no means simply to be identified with him.

In the third place, the only final condition for sharing in authentic life that the New Testament lays down is a con-

[21] *Systematic Theology*, II, pp. 169 f. and 175 f.

dition that can be formulated in complete abstraction from the event Jesus of Nazareth and all that it specifically imports. This is the clear and eloquent testimony of the parable of the Last Judgment in Matthew 25 : 31-46. The obvious intent of this parable is to make the point that the only condition a man must meet to inherit the kingdom prepared for him from the foundation of the world is that he accept God's love for himself and thereby become free to respond to the concrete needs of his neighbours as and when they are made known to him in actual encounter. The *conditionalis divinus* the New Testament establishes is not in its essential expression that one must confess faith in Jesus Christ, but that he must understand himself in the concrete situations of his existence in the authentic way that is an original possibility of his life before God. Thus, so far from being something independently significant, the demand for faith in Jesus the Christ, rightly understood, is simply a transparent means for expressing this original claim always standing against our lives.

At any rate, this seems to us to be the cumulative testimony of the three lines of evidence we have briefly summarised. They support the conclusion that the New Testament's meaning in stressing, as it does, the unique and even exclusive significance of the event Jesus of Nazareth is essentially different from the mythological claims of the "right" and the "centre." The New Testament sense of the claim "only in Jesus Christ" is not that God is only to be found in Jesus and nowhere else but that the only God who is to be found anywhere—*though he is to be found everywhere*—is the God who is made known in the word that Jesus speaks and is. In *this* sense, the words of Luther are correct exegesis : *"Und ist kein andrer Gott."*

Because this is so, we have no hesitation at all in affirming that the kerygma permits, and indeed absolutely requires, the emphasis on the radical freedom of God and of man ultimately implied by "Christ without myth." Not only is it *possible* to affirm that authentic existence can be realised apart from faith in Jesus Christ or in the Christian proclamation ; it is, in fact, *necessary* that this affirmation be made. For only when one is prepared to make it can he possibly understand the inmost meaning of faith in Jesus Christ itself.

This means the only theology that can be an adequate expression of the abiding basis of Christian faith is one in which this affirmation is unambiguously made. Our conclusion, therefore, is not only that the general position of the "left" can be justified as a tenable alternative solution, but also that there is another and far weightier reason why the otherwise untenable positions of the "right" and the "centre" are indefensible solutions. We must insist with just as much emphasis as Bultmann, although with a consistency he hardly displays, that "demythologisation is a demand of faith itself." Indeed, we must affirm with him that "radical demythologisation is the precise parallel to the Pauline-Lutheran doctrine of righteousness by faith alone without the works of the law."[22]

The tragedy of Protestant theology is that it has so seldom fully envisaged the radical implications of the Reformation principles *sola gratia—sola fide*. Although, beginning with the Reformers themselves, the one point has been well made that man is saved through faith alone in complete freedom from "works," the corresponding point about the saving action of God has almost never been grasped. It has rarely been seen that God saves man by grace alone in complete freedom from any saving "work" of the kind traditionally portrayed in the doctrines of the person and work of Jesus Christ.

To be sure, the deepest conviction of Christian faith is that God's saving action has been decisively disclosed in the event Jesus of Nazareth ; and, in this sense, Jesus is indeed God's "work" of salvation. But when this conviction is so expressed that the event of Jesus becomes a condition apart from which God is not free to be a gracious God, the heretical doctrine of

---

[22] *Kerygma und Mythos*, II, p. 207 (English translation by R. H. Fuller in H. W. Bartsch [ed.], *Kerygma and Myth*: Harper Torchbooks, 1961, pp. 210 f.).

works-righteousness achieves its final and most dangerous triumph. Instead of regarding Jesus in relation to God's grace in strict analogy to our own "works" in relation to the faith that ought properly to lie behind them, Protestant theology has generally perpetuated an unreformed christology and soteriology that are the exact counterpart of all it sets itself against in the doctrines of man and the Christian life.[23]

The historic calling of Protestantism, however, is to combat the heresy of works-righteousness in *all* the forms it assumes in the life and doctrine of the Christian church. And because this is so, Protestant theology has an even more basic warrant for rejecting the positions of the "right" and the "centre" in favour of the general position of the "left." For faith's own insistence on the freedom and transcendence of God and the freedom and responsibility of man requires precisely the kind of alternative that is also clearly demanded by our contemporary situation.

10. CHRIST WITHOUT MYTH

What remains to be done to complete the argument of the study is to set forth summarily the general constructive position that emerges as the only real alternative in the present situation. The purpose of what follows is to present by means of two main theses and a minimum of elaborative commentary the essential method and content of what we suppose to be a genuinely post-liberal theology.

　1. *Christian faith is to be interpreted exhaustively and without*

[23] One notable and encouraging exception to this generalisation is the position of Tillich. Cf. especially *Systematic Theology*, ii, pp. 175 f., where he argues, in a way parallel to our own argument, that "theology *must* make a differentiation" between the terms "in the Cross" and "through the Cross" because "the atoning processes are created by God and God alone." Obviously what Tillich means when he argues that it is not *in* but *through* the cross that atonemement is actualised is that the cross is a "work" of God in the authentic Protestant sense.

remainder as man's original possibility of authentic existence as this is clarified and conceptualised by an appropriate philosophical analysis.

This first thesis, which summarises the essential *method* of our position, records once again our complete acceptance of Bultmann's demand for demythologisation and existential interpretation. Since the essential nature of this demand as well as the reasons for accepting it have been dealt with at length in the foregoing sections, we may restrict our discussion here to two related questions requiring more consideration than we have yet given them.

The first question is whether the demythologisation we are demanding does or does not require the elimination of all "symbolic" or "analogical" language in speaking of the divine. It has been a commonly held conviction of the Western philosophical-theological tradition that God and his activity can be spoken about only in such analogical language. The reasons for this conviction have been many and varied ; and it is arguable that some of them (for example, that God is not *a* being but "being-itself" and therefore is in no sense the subject of the literal predication of basic categories) can have little force for an adequate Christian theology.[24] Still, the conviction itself, in one form or another, is so widely shared that one suspects much of the initial distrust of Bultmann's proposal has been due to his critics' supposing it contravenes this venerable theological tradition.[25]

If our earlier argument is correct, however, such distrust is misplaced, since it rests on a misunderstanding of Bultmann's view of myth and so of the meaning of demythologisation. It

[24] Cf. Charles Hartshorne, "The Idea of God—Literal or Analogical?" *Christian Scholar*, June, 1956, pp. 131-136.

[25] Cf., e.g., the statements of Reinhold Niebuhr in C. W. Kegley and R. W. Bretall (eds.), *Reinhold Niebuhr: His Religious, Social, and Political Thought*, New York: The Macmillan Company, 1956, pp. 438 f. and 446; and Paul Tillich in *Systematic Theology*, II, pp. 29 and 152, and in *Dynamics of Faith*, New York: Harper & Brothers, 1937, pp. 50 f.

will be recalled that we not only defended Bultmann's concept of myth against the charge of "ambiguity," but also rejected the claim, which was seen to be related to that charge, that, in describing his position, "it would be more accurate to speak of transmythologisation than of demythologisation."[26] This we did on the ground that if his own understanding of myth is strictly observed and is not confused with the "wider" concept admittedly more prevalent, then the meaning of demythologisation will be seen to be narrower than is often supposed and such as in no way to rule out restating the kerygma in terms of existential "analogies" distinguishable from myth.

But, as we also remarked in our earlier discussion, it is most unfortunate that Bultmann has not seen fit to develop more fully the important distinction between "analogy" and "myth" necessarily presupposed by his position. Until it is made clear (as has been done, in effect, by Charles Hartshorne[27]) that one can speak of God "analogically" without also having to speak of him "mythologically," it can hardly be expected that the demand for demythologisation will be correctly understood.

We may suggest, however, that Bultmann's failure to clarify this point is entirely of a piece with another peculiarity of his thought often noted by his critics. Perhaps the most frequently encountered criticisms of his demand for existential interpretation is that it must inevitably lead to a dissolution of theology into anthropology and to the sacrifice of faith's "objective" reference to an exclusively "subjective" interpretation. Even

---

[26] John Macquarrie, *op. cit.*, p. 176.

[27] It may be held that Hartshorne's attempt to take seriously "the religious idea of God" by interpreting it in strict analogy with personal existence represents the fulfilment of what, in Bultmann's fragmentary remarks, is hardly more than a postulate. In any event, God can be spoken about, without speaking in the inadequate manner either of mythology or of most classical ontology, only in some such way as Hartshorne proposes. Cf. especially *Man's Vision of God*, New York: Harper & Brothers, 1941.

if, as Friedrich Gogarten has rightly argued,[28] those who make this criticism generally are themselves so much the captives of a certain subject-object type of thinking as to be unable to imagine an alternative, their criticism still has point —at least in relation to *some* of Bultmann's statements. For instance, when he illicitly concludes that because, for Paul, "every assertion about God is simultaneously an assertion about man and *vice versa*," Paul's theology "is most appropriately presented as the doctrine of man,"[29] he leaves himself open to just this criticism. If the premise is correct (and this, we may note, is all existential interpretation need or may import), then one might equally well conclude that Paul's theology may best be presented as the doctrine of *God*. In any event, unless this second conclusion is also acknowledged as possible, Bultmann can scarcely dismiss it as a misunderstanding if he is accused of giving a false and one-sided emphasis to faith's assertions.

Similar remarks apply to another, much criticised statement. This is the statement that "the cross is not the salvation-event because it is the cross of Christ; it is the cross of Christ because it is the salvation-event."[30] Critics have rightly claimed that this assertion betrays an unwarranted and, we may add, quite unnecessary "subjectivism." Clearly, if the latter half of the statement is true, then the former half must be true as well—provided only that to call the cross the "salvation-event" is not a mere fiction.

To be sure, the first half of the assertion does *not* need to

[28] Cf. *Entmythologisierung und Kirche*, Stuttgart: Friedrich Vorwerk Verlag, 2nd ed., 1953, p. 110 (English translation by N. H. Smith in *Demythologising and History*, London: S.C.M. Press, Ltd., 1955, p. 85).

[29] *Theologie des Neuen Testaments*, Tübingen: J. C. B. Mohr, 3rd ed., 1958, p. 192 (English translation by Kendrick Grobel in Rudolf Bultmann, *Theology of the New Testament*, New York: Charles Scribner's Sons, 1951, 1955, Vol. 1, p. 191).

[30] H. W. Bartsch (ed.), *Kerygma und Mythos*, Vol. 1, Hamburg: Herbert Reich-Evangelischer Verlag, 2nd ed., 1951, p. 46 (English translation by R. H. Fuller in H. W. Bartsch [ed.], *Kerygma and Myth*, New York: Harper Torchbooks, 1961, p. 41).

be understood in the mistaken manner of myth or of most of Bultmann's critics on the "right." But if it is through the cross that salvation actually takes place, then *in some sense* it must be equally legitimate to say it is the cross of Christ because it saves and it saves because it is the cross of Christ. When Bultmann simply denies this, he so expresses himself as to raise a legitimate question whether he does justice to the "objective" reference of the Christian faith.

Even so, the basis for such a question is almost certainly more a fault of formulation than of substance. As our own study should be sufficient to show, Bultmann explicitly emphasises that faith has its "object," its *Woran*, and, indeed, just because this is so—or, more accurately, just because this "object" is the kind of "object" it is—radical existential interpretation becomes imperative.

Still, there are difficulties with his assurances, as becomes evident when he typically puts the word "objective" so used in quotation marks.[31] He is obviously at something of a loss in speaking about God in "objective" terms. We pointed out in Section 4 that he is unlike some of the existentialists because he consistently holds with Heidegger that there can be such a thing as an "objective" science of man's inner life. We also noted that, although he hesitates to use the word "objective" to describe such a science, he is eventually forced to use it to distinguish his position from one like Karl Jaspers' and to give content to the important methodological distinction between *existential* and *existentiell* understanding.

Nevertheless, it cannot be said that Bultmann displays a similar consistency in acknowledging that God also may be spoken about in "objective" but not "mythological" terms. On the contrary, he has even asserted self-contradictorily that to speak "about" God is meaningless and has drawn the con-

---

[31] Cf., e.g., *Kerygma und Mythos*, II, p. 196 (p. 196); and *Glauben und Verstehen*, III, p. 117.

clusion that "if one wants to speak of God, it is clear he must *speak of himself.*"[32]

To be sure, there are other passages where a different point of view is probably expressed, although the difficulty with such passages is that they are generally so confused and unclear as to make a certain judgment impossible. Consider, for example, the following:

> It is wrong to speak of God as acting in general statements, in terms of the formal analysis of man's existence. It is precisely the formal, existentialist analysis of human existence which shows that it is indeed impossible to speak of our personal existence in general statements. I can speak of my personal existence only here and now in the concrete situation of my life. To be sure, I can explicate in general statements the meaning, the sense of the conception of God and of God's action in so far as I can say that God is the power which bestows upon me life and existence, and in so far as I can describe these actions as the encounter which demands my own personal decision. By doing so I acknowledge that I cannot speak of God's action in general statements; I can speak only of what He does here and now with me, of what He speaks here and now to me. Even if we do not speak of God in general terms but rather of His action here and now on us, we must speak in terms of general conceptions, for all of our language employs conceptions, but it does not follow that the issue in hand is a general one.[33]

This passage may serve to show that Bultmann's treatment of this question is severely handicapped because he is unable to affirm consistently and, as it were, with a good conscience that God is an "object" of thought as well as the inescapable

---

[32] *Glauben und Verstehen*, Vol. 1, Tübingen: J. C. B. Mohr, 2nd ed., 1954, p. 28 (English translation by F. H. Littell in "What Sense is there to Speak of God?" *Christian Scholar*, Fall, 1960, p. 219).

[33] *Jesus Christ and Mythology*, New York: Charles Scribner's Sons, 1958, pp. 66 f. Cf. also the less confused statement in *Glauben und Verstehen*, III, pp. 120 f.

"subject" of existential encounter, and therefore may be as appropriately considered as man by philosophical analysis. In practice, of course, Bultmann implies precisely this by constantly speaking about God in terms of "analogies" drawn from Heidegger's existential philosophy. In theory, too, he implies the same thing by denying that talk about God is merely "figurative" or "symbolic" and urging instead that one may speak of God in "the fully real and 'objective' sense" by means of existential "analogies."[34]

Even so, like others of the existentialists, Bultmann is so averse to the kind of "objectification" of God by which he is robbed of his essential "subjectivity" that he turns a legitimate criticism of inadequate modes of "objectification" ("mythology," classical and German idealism, etc.) into an illegitimate condemnation of "objectification" as such.[35] In so doing, he runs the risk of a "subjectification" not only just as inadequate but equally foreign to the real substance of his position.

We are suggesting, in other words, that Bultmann's failure to develop the theory of "analogy" so essential to the adequate statement of his position *and* his tendency to speak in a one-sidedly "anthropological" or "subjective" way are both to be explained because he does not consistently acknowledge the full scope of the philosophical task. Instead of recognising that with reference to God also we can have not simply one but *two* types of understanding, namely, an *existential* one as well as an *existentiell* one (or, in different terms, a "knowledge

[34] *Kerygma und Mythos*, II, p. 196 (p. 196). It is incorrect to say with Macquarrie that Bultmann simply denies a "direct speaking of God's act" (cf. *op. cit.*, pp. 175 ff. and 240-245). Because Macquarrie completely neglects Bultmann's concept of "analogy," he presents a one-sided picture of Bultmann's rejection of "objective" talk about God.

[35] This tendency of existentialist philosophers and theologians has been well criticised by Frederick Copleston, S.J., in his analysis, of "theistic existentialism" in *Contemporary Philosophy*, London: Burns and Oates, 1956, pp. 222-227. Unfortunately, the constructive work of Fritz Buri is vulnerable to the same criticism. Cf., e.g., his several discussions of the "concept of truth" in *Dogmatik als Selbstverständnis des christlichen Glaubens*, I, *passim*.

about" as well as a "knowledge of"), he tends to see only the latter and so unduly restricts legitimate and necessary philosophical inquiry to the analysis of human existence.[36]

But this, in effect, is already to give answer to the second question we proposed to consider. If it is asked whether an existential restatement of the Christian kerygma can appropriately take place except in the terms of Heidegger's existential analysis, our answer is obviously yes. Indeed, we must insist that what Bultmann himself means by "existential interpretation" can be properly carried out only when Heidegger's analysis of *human* existence is viewed in the perspective of the general ontology it seems to imply and in which *divine* existence also is appropriately analysed and conceptualised.

Bultmann himself, in his fragmentary theory of "analogy" and, even more, in his actual practice, has pointed the way to this ampler conceptuality. But there is another resource, indigenous to our own experience and traditions, quite as important to this end as Heidegger's existentialism. This is the position of "process philosophy," especially as developed by Charles Hartshorne.[37]

Indeed, we would suggest that an adequate solution to our theological problem waits on an attempt to think through in an integral way the respective contributions of these two movements in contemporary philosophy. Until process philosophy is informed by the insights of existential analysis its lack of an explicit anthropology, which handicaps it for theological employment, can hardly be remedied in keeping

[36] Cf. his arguments that "an analysis of human existence without regard for God is not only possible, but alone makes sense" in *Kerygma und Mythos,* II, pp. 194 f. (pp. 195 f.) and *Jesus Christ and Mythology,* pp. 58 f.

[37] In addition to the writings of Hartshorne already cited, see especially *Beyond Humanism,* New York: Harper & Brothers, 1937; *The Divine Relativity,* New Haven: Yale University Press, 1948; and *Reality as Social Process,* Glencoe, Illinois: The Free Press, 1953. Also of great importance is Hartshorne's discussion with Tillich; cf. "Tillich's Doctrine of God," *The Theology of Paul Tillich,* ed. by C. W. Kegley and R. W. Bretall, New York: The Macmillan Company, 1952, pp. 164-195; and "Process as Inclusive Category: A Reply," *Journal of Philosophy,* February, 1955, pp. 94-102.

with its own implicit principles. On the other hand, unless the general ontology to which existential analysis seems to point is fully developed—and one may argue that if it is it will be only verbally distinguishable from a position like Hartshorne's[38] —existentialism will either remain an "anthropological fragment" or else be artificially engrafted on a traditional "substance" ontology that undercuts its inmost meaning (as seems to have happened in the case of Tillich).

In this sense, process philosophy also has a crucial role to play in achieving an adequate solution to the present theological problem. If a discriminating use is made of *all* the insights more recent inquiries in metaphysics have provided, the demand for existential interpretation can be more appropriately fulfilled than by depending on Heidegger's existential analysis alone.

Lest this statement be misunderstood, however, it must be emphasised we are not saying that an existential type of philosophy must be inherently incomplete and so requires to be filled out or supplemented by some more "objective" mode of thought.[39] On the contrary, we have tried to indicate that existential philosophy has its own appropriate kind of "objective" reference, and therefore the proper way to banish the ghosts of "subjectivism" and "anthropocentrism" is by clearly developing *this* "objectivity," rather than by having recourse to some alien philosophy with which existential analysis is incompatible. There is nothing to be gained in fleeing from an illusory devil of "subjectivism" only to be embraced by a real witch of "objectivism" inadequate on philosophical and theological grounds alike. This is so in spite of the counsel of despair most frequently heard from those who rightly sense the inadequacy of Bultmann's con-

[38] Cf. the brief but suggestive discussion of Heidegger's programme in *Sein und Zeit* in *Beyond Humanism*, pp. 298 ff.

[39] Cf., e.g., Geraint Vaughan Jones, *Christology and Myth in the New Testament*, New York: Harper & Brothers, 1956, pp. 268-281.

ceptuality. What is required is not some other and more "objective" philosophy, but rather the full explication of existentialism's own implicit "objectivism," for which divine and human existence alike are proper "objects" of knowledge and speech as well as "subjects" of *existentiell* encounter.

In short, the door to traditional types of "objectivism," whether "mythology" or most classical ontology, must remain closed ; and we must persist in the affirmation that "statements about God and his activity" may be interpreted without remainder as "statements about human existence." This we may do because all this affirmation need imply is that the only man and God we know anything about are, in the words of Emil Brunner, a "man-who-comes-from-God" (*Menschen-von-Gott-her*) and a "God-who-is-turned-towards-man" (*Gott-zum-Menschen-hin*).[40]

2. *Christian faith is always a "possibility in fact" because of the unconditioned gift and demand of God's love, which is the ever-present ground and end of all created things ; the decisive manifestation of this divine love, however, is the event Jesus of Nazareth, which fulfils and corrects all other manifestations and is the originative event of the church and its distinctive word and sacraments.*

This second thesis presents summarily the essential *content* of the alternative position we want to develop. The reader will note that it is already presupposed by the first thesis and, in turn, presupposes this thesis as its appropriate counterpart in the matter of theological method. It will also be noted that we have formulated both theses in such a way as to exhibit their all-but-complete agreement with the two parallel theses in which we earlier summarised the position of Bultmann. Aside from the one but fundamental difference that our theses are so stated as to overcome the structural inconsistency of Bultmann's solution, the two sets of propositions are virtually the same. This may be taken as concrete evidence of our con-

[40] Cf. *op. cit.*, p. 33 (pp. 46 f.).

viction that Bultmann has already provided the main ingredients of a genuinely post-liberal theology.

Nevertheless, because there is this basic difference and because it seems to us Bultmann does not adequately express the "objective" or indicative meaning of the decisive event of divine manifestation, there are two further comments we must make. By making them, we hope to define still more sharply the main outlines of a theology of "Christ without myth."

The first comment is that if an adequate post-liberal theology is to be developed, the doctrine of revelation must be formulated rather differently from the ways in which it has traditionally been presented. We argued earlier that it is not only possible on Scriptural grounds, but in fact necessary to affirm that authentic human existence, or faith in Christ, can be realised apart from faith in Jesus or in the specific proclamation of the church. We documented this argument, in part, by appealing to the way Paul deals with the question of man's "natural" knowledge of God in Romans 1 : 18 ff. We also implied that Paul's way of handling this matter is significantly different both from the *theologia naturalis* of traditional Catholicism and the half-hearted Catholicism of much Protestant theology. Our point was that, unlike many of his successors, Paul does *not* affirm that what is presented in God's original self-disclosure is something different from what is given in his final manifestation in Jesus of Nazareth. On the contrary, he implies that the *content* of these two forms of manifestation is and must be strictly the same, for the reason that to deny this contravenes all the-important claim that sinful men are "without excuse" for their estrangement from God.

Likewise, it would never have occurred to Paul to doubt that the righteousness of God revealed in Jesus of Nazareth had already long been attested by God's dealing with Israel and thence, as he says, through "the law and the prophets" (Rom. 3 : 21). He naturally assumes not only that men universally have the possibility of authentic existence because "what can be known of God is plain to them" in "the things that have been made" (Rom. 1 : 19 f.), but that "this possibility has especially been given to the Jew through the law, in which he daily encounters God's claim and by which he is daily led to see that he does not exist by and for himself, but that his being is limited by the claim under which he stands."[41] Paul can also argue in Romans 4 that Abraham is "the father of us all" and can summon Christians to "share the faith of Abraham," not because Abraham believed in Jesus, but because he "believed God, and it was reckoned to him as righteousness (vv. 16 and 3).

Our conviction is that the present theological problem can be adequately solved only when this Pauline and also biblical way of understanding revelation is brought to full and uninhibited expression.[42] What is required in contemporary theology is more of a sense for the wisdom of Psalm 19, which, while it gives full weight to "the law and the testimony," never forgets the speechless speech and voiceless voice by which both day and night the heavens endlessly tell the glory of God and the firmament proclaims his handiwork. We need to learn the lesson so eloquently taught a century ago by Frederick Denison Maurice, who unfailingly insisted that "Christ was before He took human flesh and dwelt among us," that "He actually conversed with prophets and patriarchs and made them aware of His presence," and that He "is in every man, the source of all light that ever visits him, the root of all the righteous thoughts and acts that he is ever able to conceive or do."[43] Maurice's witness, indeed, is so relevant for our problem that we may quote at length his commentary on the

[41] Cf. Schubert M. Ogden (ed.), *Existence and Faith: Shorter Writings of Rudolf Bultmann*, New York: Meridian Books, Inc., 1960, p. 83.

[42] Cf. C. H. Dodd, "Natural Law in the Bible," *Theology*, May, June, 1946, pp. 130-133; 161-167.

[43] *Theological Essays*, New York: Harper & Brothers, 1957, p. 60; cf. also pp. 73, 94 ff., 207 ff., and 331.

Thirteenth Article of Religion, "Of Works before Justification." This article, he argues,

> . . . cannot, of course, refer to the works done before Christ died for men's sins and rose again for their justification ; it does not concern one period of the world's history more than another. . . . "The grace of Christ, the Inspiration of His Spirit" must, it says, be the spring of every good act. Most inwardly do I accept that teaching. I know not how far the compilers of the Articles meant it to be carried. They may not have recognised the length and breadth of their own proposition. But I cannot see how we can safely take it in any limited sense. If we do and must attribute virtues to heathens, then we do and must suppose that their virtues had their source "in the grace of Christ and the Inspiration of His Spirit." Those who regard Christ as merely a man born at a certain time into this world, and the head of a sect called Christians, may stumble at such an assertion. But I need not tell you that this is not the orthodox faith; not the doctrine of these Articles. They set forth Christ "as the Son, the Word of the Father, begotten from everlasting of the Father." They say "that everlasting life is offered to mankind by Christ in the Old Testament" ; when He had not taken flesh. There is every reason therefore in the tenor of the Articles for giving this one its full import.[44]

Maurice may help us to understand that the responsibility of contemporary theology is to make clear that the hidden power, the inner meaning, the real substance, of *all* human happenings is the event of Christ. What faith means by "Christ," he rightly tells us, is not one historical event alongside others, but rather the *eschatological* event, or *eternal* word of God's unconditioned love, which is the ground and end of all historical events whatever.

[44] Quoted by Alec R. Vidler in *The Theology of F. D. Maurice,* London: S.C.M. Press, Ltd., 1948, pp. 79 f.

To be sure, the church stands by the claim that the decisive manifestation of this divine word is none other than the human word of Jesus of Nazareth and thence of its own authentic proclamation. But the point of this claim is not that the Christ is manifest only in Jesus and nowhere else, but that the word addressed to men *everywhere*, in all the events of their lives, is none other than the word spoken in Jesus and in the preaching and sacraments of the church.

One of the most pressing tasks of a post-liberal theology is so to formulate the doctrine of revelation that *this* point is made its controlling centre. This means, of course, we will have to reject all the traditional attempts to distinguish sharply between "Old Testament and New Testament," "law and gospel," "nature and grace," "philosophy and theology," "general revelation and special revelation," "reason and faith," "question and answer," "prophecy and fulfilment." In each case, such attempts finally rest back on a mythological understanding of revelation that is indefensible from the standpoint of our contemporary picture of ourselves and our world, and is also inadequate as an understanding of faith itself. Faith has nothing to gain and much to lose if it is not made unmistakably clear that no other word is spoken in Jesus than is everywhere spoken in the actual events of nature and history and specifically witnessed to with more or less adequacy by "the law and the prophets."

Another important implication is that we must think through afresh the whole problem of the relationship between faith in Jesus Christ and the various mythologies, philosophies, and religions in which the perennial question of human existence and its equally perennial answer have found expression. We have reached a point where most of the solutions to this problem proposed by Christian theology can, for different reasons, no longer be maintained ; and the prospect of "the coming world civilisation" and all it portends lends a special urgency to this phase of our task. Suffice it to say that a tenable solution to the problem will be required to accord a far more positive significance to man's various attempts to understand his existence than has generally been accorded to them by Protestant theology. We must be guided by the thoughts recently well expressed by the Marburg historian Ernst Benz :

> . . . if history is in a sense the history of salvation, then this history cannot have begun with Moses in 1250 B.C. The history of salvation is as old as the history of mankind, which we assume is some 6,000,000 years older than Moses. And if this is so, then the history of religions and the history of the development of the religious consciousness must be seen as coterminous with the history of salvation. If the revelation in Christ is really the fulfilment of time, then it must also be the fulfilment of the history of religions. Then, also, the earlier stages of religion which mankind passed through stand in a meaningful and positive relation to this fulfilment of time and of the history of mankind. On this basis, one of the most important tasks of contemporary Christian scholarship would be to set forth a new theology of the history of religions.[45]

If such a task is to be accomplished, we must rid ourselves of the notion that mankind's several attempts at self-understanding express merely the "question" for God[46] and recognise rather that they also reflect the *answer* to that question, if only in ways that, from the standpoint of the word spoken in Jesus, are fragmentary and inadequate—and even false. This will be all the more possible the sooner we recognise that, so far from

---

[45] "On Understanding the Non-Christian Religions," *Midway*, July, 1960, p. 45. Benz rightly recognises that his views were also profoundly shared by the late Joachim Wach. Cf., e.g., Wach's address, "General Revelation and the Religions of the World," *Journal of Bible and Religion*, April, 1954, pp. 83-93.

[46] So Bultmann in *Existence and Faith*, pp. 89 f.; cf. also *Glauben und Verstehen*, II, pp. 79-104, 117-132 (pp. 90-118, 133-150).

excluding a "natural" knowledge of God, the fact of mankind's universal sinfulness actually presupposes it. The reason men can be addressed as sinners and be confronted with the promise of forgiveness manifested in Jesus is that, although they know God, they exchange the truth about him for a lie, and worship and serve the creature rather than the Creator. If this insight is taken seriously and we constantly remember the deep truth that *anima humana naturaliter Christiana*, we should be able to make a most significant contribution to a more adequate Protestant theology.

Our second comment is that, for the reasons discussed above, Bultmann's existential interpretation fails to express in an adequate way the "objective" reality of the revelatory event Jesus the Christ. This comment is not only underscored by several of Bultmann's critics (although, naturally, in ways that generally betray the inadequate position of the "right"), but is also fully justified by certain of his own statements. We have already mentioned the one statement in which he falsely opposes the "subjective" or soteriological significance of the cross for faith to its "objective" or christological reality as the decisive revelatory occurrence. He implies a similar view in the questions he raises in critically evaluating "the christological confession of the World Council of Churches."[47] "To what extent," he asks, "is a christological statement about [Christ] simultaneously a statement about me ? Does he help me because he is the Son of God, or is he the Son of God because he helps me ?"

Bultmann apparently wants us to understand that the alternative posed by the second sentence points to two opposed ways of understanding Jesus Christ between which one is forced to choose. But such a view must be rejected. For, even though every "statement about Christ" *is* a "statement about me," the event of Christ can be the event through which "help" or salvation is given only because it is the kind of

---

[47] *Glauben und Verstehen,* II, p. 252 (p. 280).

event it actually is—or, in other words, because *in some sense* Christ is in very truth "the Son of God."

That Bultmann himself in fact recognises this in most of the things he says will be perfectly evident to anyone who listens sympathetically to what he wants to say. In this very essay, for example, he makes clear that Jesus Christ is the "eschatological event" even for unfaith, although in this case the meaning of the event is judgment rather than salvation.[48] Even so, because he is so unqualifiedly averse to "objectification" as necessarily falsifying the meaning of faith, he is unable to express consistently and appropriately in a non-mythological way the "objective" reality of the decisive revelatory event. Therefore, however unjust and one-sided, the familiar criticisms that he dissolves christology into soteriology or indicative into imperative cannot be dismissed as having no point.

But the lesson to be learned from such criticisms is quite different than those who make them would like to suppose. What we must learn is not that we need some other and more "objective" christology, but that we must carry forward Bultmann's own existential interpretation by expressing more adequately than he himself has done the "objective" reality of the event Jesus Christ that such interpretation implies.

The present context is not the place to undertake this task. But there could hardly be a more fitting way to conclude our study than by briefly suggesting certain considerations that would be important in carrying it out. Two considerations in particular ought to be mentioned.

First of all, the entire reality of Jesus of Nazareth, including not only his preaching and acts of healing, but his fellowship with sinners and his eventual death on the cross, was transparent to the word he sought to proclaim. By this is meant that the event of Jesus, in its parts and as a whole, is a *"historical"* (*geschichtlich*) event in the sense clarified by Bultmann—

[48] *Ibid.*, p. 258 (p. 286).

that is, an event that in its "significance" confronts those who encounter it with a certain possibility of *existentiell* understanding. Thus, Jesus' table fellowship with harlots and publicans has the most profound connection with his proclamation of the imminent reign of God. What is proclaimed in words in the parables of the Lost Sheep and the Lost Coin and the Lost Son in Luke 15 is dramatically signified in action by Jesus' own associations with the "lost" among his contemporaries.[49] Similarly, his healings are explicitly understood by him as "signs" of God's coming reign (cf. Luke 11 : 20 ; Matt. 12 : 28 ; 11 : 4 ff.). And even his crucifixion itself, as Bultmann rightly emphasises, powerfully re-raises the same question of decision raised by his preaching. The cross simply presents in a definitive way the possibility of self-understanding for which his entire life was the transparent means of expression.

The *content* of this possibility—in Bultmann's terms, its "what"—is nothing other than man's ontological possibility of authentic historical existence. In summoning men to live in radical dependence on God's grace, and so in freedom from the past and openness to the future, the event of Jesus is but the re-presentation in the form of a single human life of man's original possibility of existence *coram deo*. Indeed, in its non-mythological sense, Jesus' office as the Christ consists precisely in his being the bearer, through word and deed and tragic destiny, of the eternal word of God's love, which is the transcendent meaning of all created things and the final event before which man must decide his existence.[50]

That these remarks say nothing different from what can easily be found in the New Testament may be so obvious that

[49] Cf. Günther Bornkamm, *Jesus von Nazareth*, Stuttgart: W. Kohlhammer Verlag, pp. 73 f. (English translation by James M. Robinson, *et al.* in Günther Bornkamm, *Jesus of Nazareth*, Harper & Brothers, 1960, pp. 80 f.)

[50] Cf. Rudolf Bultmann, *Jesus*, Tübingen: J. C. B. Mohr, 3rd ed., 1951, pp. 177-182. (English translation by L. P. Smith and E. H. Lantero in Rudolf Bultmann, *Jesus and the Word*, New York: Charles Scribner's Sons, 2nd ed., 1958, pp. 212-219.)

our making them seems unnecessary. Yet the fact that well-meaning interpreters still insist on speaking of Jesus' "numinous personality" and attempt in this way to explain his significance for the apostolic faith may caution us against assuming too hastily that our remarks are as commonplace as they seem.[51] The legacy of a mythological understanding of Jesus and of other equally inadequate types of "objectifying" his reality as the Christ is so much with us that a clear grasp of the New Testament's meaning is not readily achieved.

Still, what such inadequate formulations intend to express is the central conviction of the apostolic witness—that in the event Jesus of Nazareth something of ultimate significance for the whole history of mankind has been manifested. Where most traditional theology has gone astray, however, is in so speaking of this event as to suggest it is something other than the historically decisive disclosure of the very truth that, in the words of the propers for Christmas day, God "at sundry times and in divers manners spake in time past unto the fathers by the prophets" and, even beyond this, "lighteth every man that cometh into the world." The New Testament, by contrast, is much clearer in its testimony that what has taken place in Jesus of Nazareth is nothing more and nothing less than a definitive re-presentation of man's existence before God that has all the force of final revelation.

The import of this first consideration, however, may be made more understandable by presenting the second. It belongs to the nature of a true statement that, just insofar as it is true, it is transparent to the reality that makes it true. Indeed, *this reality itself is actually present "in, with, and under" the statement that seeks to express it.* When we say, then, that the integral significance of the event of Jesus is to re-present as a possibility demanding decision the final truth about man's existence *coram deo*, we are actually saying the reality this

---

[51] Cf., e.g., John Macquarrie, *op. cit.*, pp. 23, 80 and 179; and Geraint Vaughan Jones, *op. cit.*, pp. 122 and 163.

truth seeks to express is literally present "in, with, and under" that same event.

In other words, the full "objective" reality of this event is something infinitely more than merely a human life and a human word of witness. The reason we can speak of it as the "eschatological event" *pro se, extra nos, sine nobis, et contra nos* is that in its deepest reaches it is nothing less than the God-man relationship that is the essential reality of every human life. By this is meant not that Jesus himself in his "person" actualises this relationship *existentiell*,[52] but rather that the word he speaks and is, in fulfilling his "office," is the re-presentation *to us* of the possibility of such a relationship. What has happened once for all and with entire sufficiency by his presence among us is the decisive statement of the ultimate truth "in, with, and under" which the reality to which that statement corresponds is literally and verily present. Therefore, the present proclamation of the church, whether as *verbum audibile* or *verbum visibile*, is simply the re-presentation here and now of the event of Jesus, which, in turn, is completely transparent to "the Christ," to the final reality of God's love that confronts us as sovereign gift and demand in all the events of our existence.

In speaking in this way, we may be misunderstood as simply re-stating the christology widely characteristic of the earlier liberal theology.[53] It may be supposed the "objectivity" we have in mind when we speak of Jesus as the definitive statement of the truth about God and man is essentially the same as that to which the liberal theologians also referred when they spoke of Jesus' "teachings" and presented him as the great "teacher" of the human race.

Such a supposition, however, would be quite mistaken. Although we agree with the liberal theologians that the only

[52] Cf. the contrary position of Tillich, *Systematic Theology*, II, pp. 148 ff., and Friedrich Schleiermacher, *The Christian Faith*, ed. by H. R. Mackintosh and J. S. Stewart, Edinburgh: T. & T. Clark, 1928, pp. 377-424.

[53] Cf. *Kerygma und Mythos*, I, pp. 24 f. (pp. 13 f.).

"objectivity" about Jesus of which the New Testament itself intends to speak is one that has its basis in the word he proclaims and is, we want to make much clearer than they generally did that his proclamation is not a body of timeless truths, but an *existentiell* communication demanding decision. The purpose of Jesus' ministry, whether of word or deed, was far less to speak *about* man and his relationship to God—although he did that, too—than to speak *of* that relationship so that it itself could be encountered in its full existential reality. It was much the same as when a father seeks to say to a disobedient son that his offence is forgiven. The father's purpose in speaking is not to talk *about* his forgiveness and the new relationship it makes possible, but rather to speak *of* his forgiveness or to bestow it, so as actually to establish such a relationship. Likewise, when Jesus speaks of the forgiveness of God, his intention is not to describe it to the theoretical intellect, but, as one who is "sent" or authorised by God, actually to bestow it as an *existentiell* possibility.

Therefore, we should argue that the *conditio sine qua non* for a more adequate christology is to observe the important distinction between "knowledge about" and "knowledge of," or, in Bultmann's terms, *existential* and *existentiell* understanding. The statement that Jesus is the decisive re-presentation of the truth of man's existence can be appropriately clarified only when it is recognised that "truth" here is not the timeless truth of "knowledge about," but the *existentiell* truth of "knowledge of." What confronts us in Jesus is not, in its first intention, a "world-view" addressed to our intellects, but a possibility of self-understanding that requires of us a personal decision.

While we may hesitate, then, to say that Jesus is mankind's "teacher," we may confidently affirm he is its "preacher." For the office of the preacher, of which his ministry is both the norm and the fulfilment, is not only to say "what" man's existence is—although that, too, is most certainly involved—

but to speak in such a way that "what" he says becomes the occasion for an actual *existentiell* encounter with the "that" in which the "what" is grounded and to which it primarily refers.

If the question is raised whether Jesus is *only* a preacher, we may reply that the real difficulties lie less with an affirmative answer to the question than with the debased conception of the preaching office that the question itself presupposes. For, as Bultmann tells us with evident New Testament warrant (cf. e.g., II Cor. 5 : 20 ; John 13 : 20), "even the *incarnation* as the eschatological event is not a datable event of the past, but an event that occurs here and now in the proclamation." "A man like myself speaks God's word to me ; the logos of God becomes incarnate in him."[54] It is because Luther takes so seriously just such an exalted conception of the preacher's role that he can say quite naturally not only that all Christians are "Christs to one another and do to our neighbours as Christ does to us," but also that "nor was Christ sent into the world for any other ministry except that of the Word."[55]

Be this as it may, however, to say that Jesus is the preacher of mankind in the sense of the decisive historical manifestation of the essential God-man relationship is to say something quite different than that he is an accidental occasion through which some timeless and impersonal truth can be appropriated by the intellect. Indeed, it is to say nothing less, though also nothing more, than that in him the eternal Existence or Thou in whom all truth is grounded is himself personally present. In this sense, we may affirm with John Knox that "Jesus did not bring a new idea ; rather, in him an old idea ceased being an idea at all and became a living reality. As he talked about the love of God, the love of God itself drew near."[56]

[54] *Kerygma und Mythos*, II, p. 206, n. 1 (p. 209, n. 1).

[55] Harold J. Grimm (ed.), *Luther's Works*, Vol. xxxi, Philadelphia: Muhlenberg Press, 1957, pp. 368, 346.

[56] *Christ the Lord*, New York: Harper & Brothers, 1945, pp. 52 f. Knox's other writings also (especially *On the Meaning of Christ*, New York: Charles

It may appear that the argument we have sought to develop, especially in this final chapter, is nothing more than a somewhat ingenious *tour de force* in which we have made a virtue out of necessity by pretending to discover some hidden and, as it were, pre-established harmony between the demands of the *evangelium aeternum* and the exigencies of our particular situation. This is, of course, a possible, and perhaps, finally, even the *only* possible way to evaluate our argument. Nevertheless, the deep conviction we have tried to express is not apt to be shaken by any merely trifling criticisms of what may be regarded as an unusual point of view. For, so far from being persuaded that we have at last reached a stage in Christian history where we must sacrifice either faith or understanding so as not to be false to one or the other or both, we are convinced by what seem to us to be good reasons that there are opportunities confronting theology to-day perhaps unparalleled in the entire history of the church.

Scribner's Sons, 1947, and *The Death of Christ*, New York: Abingdon Press, 1958) are most significant resources for a post-liberal christology.

John Macquarrie's
"The Scope of Demythologising"

Of the studies of Bultmann's theology that have so far appeared in English, probably the most significant is the recent book by John Macquarrie, *The Scope of Demythologising : Bultmann and His Critics*.[1]   Like its earlier companion volume, *An Existentialist Theology : A Comparison of Heidegger and Bultmann*,[2] this book does much to advance the more adequate understanding of Bultmann's proposal and to facilitate its critical appropriation by English-speaking readers.   Moreover, the book picks up and carries even further the essentially constructive concern already evident in its predecessor.   Although the bulk of its contents consists in an illuminating discussion of the relation of Bultmann's theology to the criticisms of the "right" and the "left," the aim of such discussion is in no sense narrowly historical or critical.   Rather, Macquarrie's ultimate purpose is to fix the "scope" of demythologising and, in so doing, to sketch in the outlines of the kind of theological alternative he regards as adequate for the contemporary situation.

In all this, there are, of course, obvious parallels to the basic structure and concern of the present study.   The problems of the two books are precisely the same, and even in their main

[1] New York: Harper & Brothers, 1961.
[2] London: S.C.M. Press, Ltd., 1955.

principles of organisation and procedure the reader can hardly fail to note significant similarities between them.

In spite of such formal parallelism, however, the differences between the studies, so far as their *content* is concerned, are almost equally striking. As in his earlier volume, to which critical reference has been made throughout our study, Macquarrie develops a position that at several points is basically at odds with the one developed above. In fact, with the publication of this second volume, the differences between the two positions have been increased; for in the one significant respect in which the second book departs from the first—namely, in its revised judgment concerning the consistency of Bultmann's proposal—it comes into direct conflict with the argument presented in Section 8.

There is more than sufficient reason, therefore, for a critical examination of the arguments of Macquarrie's book. Such examination is made all the more imperative because of the representative character of these arguments. So far from being simply one more contribution to the English-speaking discussion of Bultmann's work, Macquarrie's book beautifully sums up the majority point of view in that discussion. Accordingly, anyone who, like the present writer, is constrained to dissent from that point of view cannot but experience Macquarrie's work as a challenge.

For both of these reasons, we propose to examine in some detail the chief points at issue between the arguments of the present study and those advanced by Macquarrie. The topics to be considered may be appropriately arranged under three general headings, which directly correspond with the three basic divisions of our larger discussion.

I. THE PROBLEM OF UNDERSTANDING
BULTMANN'S PROPOSAL

The first issue to be considered under this initial heading is *Bultmann's concept of "myth" and "analogy."* In his second book, even as in the first, Macquarrie takes the position that Bultmann's use of myth is "confused."[3] To be sure, the argument he offers in support of this position is not exactly the same as the one offered in his earlier discussion. In response to Bultmann's own reply to his previous objection, he concedes the point (also made in the present study) that Bultmann's usage can hardly be regarded as ambiguous because it embraces "cosmology" (or "primitive science") as well as what Macquarrie earlier spoke of as "myth proper."[4] Macquarrie now recognises that Bultmann's concept is in fact free of any such confusion, because, as Bultmann himself everywhere defines and uses it, it means something essentially different from what is properly spoken of as "cosmology."

But there are other objections, he feels, that make the charge of confusion seem pretty convincing. Specifically, there are three criticisms made by other English-speaking interpreters that all point to ambiguity in Bultmann's concept.[5]

First, there is the objection by Ronald W. Hepburn that Bultmann's formal definition of myth is too wide. Its sense, Hepburn claims, is "sufficiently extended to include every kind of oblique language," and so Bultmann's subsequent distinction between "myth" and "analogy" is bound to seem "a procedure for which his definition gives no warrant."[6]

---

[3] *The Scope of Demythologising*, pp. 199 ff.

[4] Cf. *ibid.*, p. 212. It may be of interest to note that Bultmann's reply to Macquarrie, which was made in a letter to him, is all but verbally identical with the one suggested above on p. 30 on the basis of an analysis of one of Bultmann's published statements.

[5] Cf. *ibid.*, pp. 200 f.

[6] Antony Flew and Alasdair Macintyre (eds.), *New Essays in Philosophical Theology*, London: S.C.M. Press, Ltd., 1955, p. 237; cf. also pp. 229 f.

Second, there is the opposite criticism of Ian Henderson's (which Macquarrie himself also urges in *An Existentialist Theology*[7]) that Bultmann's concept is too narrow. What Henderson has in mind are such "non-transcendent myths" as "the Nazi myths of blood and soil," which can hardly be included within the scope of Bultmann's definition.[8] Finally, Macquarrie refers to the claim of H. P. Owen that Bultmann's use of "myth" "makes it little more than a label for designating a very heterogeneous collection of items."[9] In particular, Owen argues, "there is a prima facie difference between miracles and a spatial notion of divine transcendence. The one is a fact and the other is the symbolisation of a fact."[10]

Having simply cited these criticisms, then, Macquarrie remarks that "it certainly appears that Hepburn is right in pointing to confusion in Bultmann's central concept" and concludes that Bultmann's "formal definition of myth must be scrapped."[11]

What is to be said of this conclusion? In the first place, it is difficult to regard it as a "conclusion" at all, since the mere citation of objections without any argument for their validity can hardly be accepted as evidence for so drastic a judgment. Of course, the reason Macquarrie can make the judgment is because he is convinced of the validity of the criticisms. But —and this is the second thing to be said—each of the criticisms is in fact open to the most serious objection in the light of a careful analysis of Bultmann's view. Indeed, the irrelevance of one of the criticisms—namely, Henderson's—has already been shown by our previous criticism of Macquarrie's own original position.[12] And the other objections as well can hardly sustain the charge that Bultmann's concept is confused.

---

[7] Cf. p. 167; cf. also above, pp. 28 ff.
[8] Cf. *Myth in the New Testament*, London: S.C.M. Press, Ltd., 1952, p. 54.
[9] *The Scope of Demythologising*, p. 200; italics deleted.
[10] *Revelation and Existence: A Study in the Theology of Rudolf Bultmann*, Cardiff: University of Wales Press, 1957, p. 5.
[11] *The Scope of Demythologising*, p. 201.   [12] Cf. above, pp. 29 f.

Thus, Owen's claim loses all plausibility as soon as one recognises his transparent misrepresentation of Bultmann's intention and gives due regard to the full implications of Bultmann's understanding of "myth." Obviously, Bultmann would never think of denying the difference between a miraculous *event* and a spatial *notion* of the divine transcendence. What he does insist on is that the manner of representation in which the divine activity is represented as "miracle" (*Mirakel* as distinguished from *Wunder*) is one and the same with that presupposed by the notion of God's spatial transcendence. Therefore, the reason he can include "miracle" within the terms of his formal definition of "myth" without confusion is because miracle involves the same "objectification" of the divine reality and action that is myth's chief defining characteristic. Only because Owen fails to see this can he claim that, as Bultmann uses it, "myth" is simply a loose designation for a heterogeneous collection of "meaningless elements."

An equally conclusive reply may be given to the objection of Hepburn. As we have already noted,[13] Hepburn makes a fatal mistake when he assumes that Bultmann's formal definition of myth is "sufficiently wide in its scope to include all pictorial, analogical and symbolical speech whatsoever."[14] He makes this mistake because he gives insufficient attention to the precise technical meaning of the terms in Bultmann's definition. When Bultmann says that "mythology is that manner of representation in which the unworldly and divine appears as the worldly and human," the pivotal word "world" is obviously being used with the same restricted meaning it almost invariably has throughout his writings. That is, it is understood to refer to what he otherwise speaks of as the realm of the "objective," which he sharply distinguishes from the realm of human existence or of man's distinctively personal life.[15]

[13] Cf. above, p. 91, n. 214. [14] *Op. cit.*, p. 229. [15] Cf. above, pp. 48 ff.

But it is just this important restriction of meaning that Hepburn overlooks. In part, perhaps, because he relies solely on the English translation of Bultmann's essay, he simply assumes that Bultmann's sense of "world" is as extensive as in ordinary English, and so, of course, has no difficulty in concluding that Bultmann's definition of myth is as "wide" as he claims. Once it is recognised that this is not the case at all, the restricted scope of Bultmann's definition can be easily grasped, and one has no trouble in understanding that his distinction between "myth" and "analogy" is a thoroughly warranted procedure.[16]

Our verdict is that Macquarrie is mistaken when he claims that Bultmann's concept of myth is "confused" and that the formal definition of the term can only be "scrapped." However useful on other grounds one may regard his attempts to "reconstruct" Bultmann's concept, his criticism of Bultmann must be rejected and the conclusion reached earlier in the study once again affirmed : Bultmann's concept is thoroughly consistent and remains completely untouched by the charge of ambiguity.

To this we may add a brief comment about Macquarrie's understanding of Bultmann's concept of "analogy."[17] Macquarrie rightly points out that Bultmann's discussion of this concept is most inadequate and that what he means by it is far from completely clear. But one must raise the question whether Bultmann's meaning is really as unclear as Macquarrie wants to hold. Bultmann has surely said enough to remove any doubt that "analogy" is to be sharply distinguished from "myth" and that the ground for the distinction lies in the correspondingly sharp difference between the realm of the "objective" and the realm of the "existential."[18] There is no indication in his writings that he means by "analogy" what Macquarrie takes him to mean. Indeed, what Macquarrie

[16] Cf. above, pp. 146 f.   [17] Cf. *The Scope of Demythologising,* pp. 202-206.
[18] Cf. above, pp. 90-93.

understands by "analogy" is what Bultmann himself consistently refers to by such words as "symbol" or "figure" (*Bild*) or "cipher"—namely, terms that were once "mythological," but are now no longer used with their original mythological meaning.[19] It is in distinction from all such terms, which even as "symbols" still have the form of "objective" mythological representations, that Bultmann speaks of "analogy"—that is, a way of speaking of God and his action which makes use solely of the personalistic concepts of existential analysis. Thus it is not at all surprising that, in his correspondence with Macquarrie, Bultmann can talk not only about demythologising, but also about "desymbolising" (*Entsymbolisierung*).[20] For what he almost certainly means by this is that "symbols," too, must be interpreted so far as possible by existential "analogies," lest their mythological form obscure their (now) non-mythological meaning.

The reason Macquarrie fails to see this is because, in a most un-Bultmannian fashion, he allows only a verbal distinction between "analogy" and "symbol." It is also for this reason, in part, that he misunderstands Bultmann's "astonishing assertion" that analogical talk does not "necessarily" involve "symbols or images." As the German parallel to this assertion makes much clearer[21] (Bultmann's English version is admittedly confusing), its point is not that "analogical" language is "direct" in the sense of not involving "analogy," but that such language does not have to be simply "symbolic," and so

[19] Cf., e.g., H. W. Bartsch (ed.), *Kerygma und Mythos*, Vol. II, Hamburg: Herbert Reich-Evangelischer Verlag, 1952, pp. 185 ff; also H. W. Bartsch (ed.), *Kerygma und Mythos*, Vol. I, Hamburg: Herbert Reich-Evangelischer Verlag, 2nd ed., 1951, p. 122 (English translation by R. H. Fuller in H. W. Bartsch [ed.], *Kerygma and Myth*, New York: Harper Torchbooks, 1961, pp. 102 f.); and Rudolf Bultmann, *Jesus Christ and Mythology*, New York: Charles Scribner's Sons, 1958, pp. 67-70. In this last book, the word Bultmann himself chooses to translate "*Bild*" is not "figure" but "image."

[20] Cf. *The Scope of Demythologising*, p. 205, n. 1.

[21] Cf. *Kerygma und Mythos*, II, p. 196 (English translation by R. H. Fuller in H. W. Bartsch [ed.], *Kerygma and Myth*, New York: Harper Torchbooks, 1961, p. 196).

is in *that* sense "direct"—that is, a real speaking about God's act, albeit in the legitimate mode of existential analogy, rather than in the misleading manner of myth.

A second issue Macquarrie poses has to do with what he speaks of as *"Bultmann's conception of modernity."*[22] He attempts to show that Bultmann's concept of modernity is "ambiguous" and "un-critical" because it sometimes includes not only the modern scientific world-picture, but also the "secularised self-understanding" so widely prevalent in the modern world. It is because of this second element, he argues, that Bultmann's theology contains so many gratuitous "concessions" to the modern man, which obscure its true intention by making it seem far more radical than it is.

There is a certain plausibility about this argument, but that it is an adequate interpretation of Bultmann's view must be seriously questioned for at least two reasons. First, it gives no indication of having taken into account what Bultmann himself says concerning the place of modern man's self-understanding in a conception of modernity. As we showed in our earlier discussion,[23] Bultmann does indeed include such self-understanding in what he means by modern thinking. But, as we also showed, he does this only under quite specific conditions. The one thing he insists theology must take seriously is modern man's understanding of himself as a closed inner unity, with its implication that "the only divine speaking and acting [man to-day] can understand as important and of concern to him are such as encounter him in his personal existence."[24] This obviously leaves open the possibility, however, of an appropriate representation of God's act as an event of personal existence, and so involves no concession whatever to a "secularised" self-understanding. Second, so far from containing "concessions" to modern secularism, Bult-

---

[22] Cf. *The Scope of Demythologising*, pp. 230-240.
[23] Cf. above, pp. 31 f., 35 ff. [24] *Kerygma und Mythos*, II, p. 182.

mann's writings are in fact filled with explicit criticisms of the "scientific world-view," which precisely parallel Macquarrie's own critical arguments.[25] That Macquarrie should not even refer to such criticisms is itself an indication of the inadequacy of his interpretation.

Related to this second issue is a third one of even greater importance. This has to do with *the basic motivation of Bultmann's theology*. Like so many other interpreters, Macquarrie takes the position that Bultmann is basically an "apologist," that the primary motive of his work is to recommend the Christian kerygma to the peculiarly modern situation. Thus, when he attempts to account for what he describes as "Bultmann's negations," he appeals solely to Bultmann's alleged "concessions" to a secularised understanding of existence.

The trouble with such a position is that it completely disregards Bultmann's own repeated statements as to the basis of his theology. The reason he himself assigns as fundamental for his project is "faith itself," that is, the understanding of man before God that he holds is implicit in faith in the kerygma of the church. We have argued elsewhere[26] that this explanation of Bultmann's method is thoroughly in keeping with the structure of his thought and is the only way to do justice to his actual mode of procedure. What accounts for his so-called "negations" is far less the exigency of the apologetic situation (although it is certainly their *occasion*) than his basic understanding of the Christian faith. Because Macquarrie simply ignores this, however, his representation of Bultmann's intention is at best quite one-sided. He is unable to recognise that what really makes Bultmann's demand for demythologising

[25] Cf., e.g., *ibid.*, pp. 187 f., 208 (p. 211); also Schubert M. Ogden (ed.), *Existence and Faith: Shorter Writings of Rudolf Bultmann*, New York: Meridian Books, Inc., 1960, pp. 206-225, especially 209 ff.; and *Glauben und Verstehen*, Vol. II, Tübingen: J. C. B. Mohr, 1952, pp. 15 ff., 77 (English translation by J. C. G. Greig in Rudolf Bultmann, *Essays, Philosophical and Theological*, London: S.C.M. Press, Ltd., 1955, pp. 17 ff., 87 f.).

[26] Cf. *Existence and Faith*, pp. 18 f.; cf. also above, pp. 43 f., 115.

so "radical" and unlimited is not his capitulation to modernity, but his fundamental grasp of the Christian kerygma itself.

This brings us to the most important issue Macquarrie raises by his understanding of Bultmann's proposal—namely, the way he interprets what he calls *"the limit to demythologising."* He claims not only that there is such a limit in Bultmann's proposal (that is, a limit to thorough-going existential interpretation) but that it is "a limit which has been set by Bultmann himself."[27] Unlike his critics on the "left"—notably Fritz Buri and Karl Jaspers—Bultmann refuses to follow the road of demythologising to its final destination and insists rather that existential interpretation must be limited by reference both to a saving act of God and to a unique historical revelation of this divine action. To be sure, Macquarrie sometimes speaks as if the setting of this limit is not so much something Bultmann explicitly does as a necessary implication of some of his central affirmations[28]; and to this extent, Macquarrie's view is ambiguous. But in yet other places, one can hardly mistake his intention to affirm that the limit to demythologising is a limit Bultmann himself quite deliberately and explicitly sets. Thus, for example, in the little allegory with which he begins his book, the whole point is that "at the last moment, as it appears," Bultmann intentionally turns aside from the way of demythologising to follow "a different road in quite a new direction."[29]

In at least one place in *An Existentialist Theology*, Macquarrie seems to make a similar claim.[30] But we have already pointed out that, like the parallel claims of certain others, it cannot be sustained by an analysis of Bultmann's proposal. We showed not only that Bultmann nowhere explicitly affirms a limit to demythologising, but that the whole purpose of the concluding section of the programmatic essay, as well as many

---

[27] *The Scope of Demythologising*, p. 11.
[28] Cf., e.g., *ibid.*, p. 223.   [29] Cf. *ibid.*, p. 11.
[30] Cf. above, pp. 76 f.; cf. also *An Existentialist Theology*, p. 174.

other statements, is explicitly to deny that any such limit needs to be set.[31]

To be sure, we argued in Section 8 that Bultmann in fact implies such a limit when he makes the claim that authentic existence is factually possible only as faith in Jesus Christ or in the kerygma of the church. But the point of our argument is that Bultmann *implies* such a limit—*not* that he explicitly sets it. Indeed, the very reason we spoke of the inconsistency of his proposal is because, in contradiction to all his explicit statements, he implicitly sets a limit to demythologising by the way he interprets the exclusivistic claim of the Christian kerygma. In our view, then, when Macquarrie claims that there is a limit to demythologising set by Bultmann himself, he obscures the fact that, although this is indeed the *implication* of Bultmann's theology, Bultmann nowhere acknowledges such a limit, and in fact explicitly denies it.

The trouble here seems to be that Macquarrie is misled by what we may call his "preunderstanding" of Bultmann's proposal. In keeping with his own constructive position, he imposes on Bultmann's view an explicitness and self-consciousness concerning the limit to demythologising that Bultmann himself completely lacks. That this is so is clearly indicated by the way he interprets Bultmann's "at first startling" assertion that "the question of God and the question of myself are identical."[32] According to Macquarrie, what Bultmann means by this is that "if religion always involves human existence, then a religious question must be at least in part an existential question."[33] Surely this is not at all what Bultmann means. He does not say that the religious question is *in part* an existential question, but that *the two questions are in fact one and the same*!

One may share Macquarrie's view that such an assertion is "dangerous" and that it has to be "supplemented" by con-

---

[31] Cf. also above, pp. 112-116. [32] *Jesus Christ and Mythology*, p. 53.
[33] *The Scope of Demythologising*, p. 43.

siderations falling outside of its exclusively existentialist scope. But that one may claim that this is *Bultmann's* view of the matter is an entirely different question. Bultmann never affirms, but rather consistently denies, that existential interpretation stands in need of any such supplementation. Therefore, when Macquarrie suggests that it is only because Bultmann sets a limit to demythologising that he can claim that faith "can now properly assert itself,"[34] what Bultmann says is misrepresented. What Bultmann holds to be justified by "faith itself" is not simply some "limited" demythologising, but rather the kind of demythologising he himself chooses to describe as "radical."[35]

In other words, in his most fundamental defence of his entire undertaking, Bultmann explicitly claims that the demythologising he is demanding is subject to no such limitation as Macquarrie alleges. That he is in fact unable to maintain this claim because of the contradictory implication of certain of his other assertions can hardly be doubted. But that Macquarrie is correct in holding that he does not intend to make the claim receives no support whatever from a careful analysis of his writings.

This leads to a final comment concerning another issue Macquarrie poses by his interpretation. In his discussion of *Bultmann's understanding of the "solus Christus,"* Macquarrie takes the position that Bultmann's view is so "equivocal" that it is difficult to know whether he does or does not maintain that God never addresses men through any other vehicle than the Christian kerygma.[36] Macquarrie notes that "Bultmann occasionally uses the word 'exclusive' and speaks as if there could be no genuine knowledge of God or of man's authentic existence apart from the Christian revelation." But he goes on to add that "Bultmann is highly ambiguous on these matters. We find him also saying that it is 'turning from the world'

---

[34] *Ibid.*, p. 22.   [35] Cf. *Kerygma und Mythos*, II, p. 207 (pp. 210 f.).
[36] Cf. *The Scope of Demythologising*, pp. 182, 184.

which is the way to God, and that Christians and non-Christians who have taken this step are unified in a 'community of the transcendent' which has nothing exclusive about it! "[37]   Macquarrie's own inclination, clearly, is to resolve the ambiguity in the direction of the latter assertion, for, in another place, he argues that "neither Bultmann nor any reasonable person would wish to gainsay" that "there is grace outside of the Christian religion" and that "men 'turn from the world' and are 'liberated' apart from the *kerygma*."[38]   Even so, Macquarrie does not attempt to force such a resolution, but is content to affirm that Bultmann's view remains ambiguous.

It will be obvious from our previous discussion that at this point also Macquarrie's position is directly opposed to the one taken in the present study.[39]   We have argued not only that Bultmann's view in this respect is quite unequivocal, but that it has a precisely opposite meaning from the one Macquarrie is inclined to give it.   The important point, however, is that this argument has been developed with full awareness of the only two passages to which Macquarrie refers in support of his contrary interpretation.   What he fails to observe is that, when these passages are read in the light of their context, they have a different meaning than he assigns them.

Thus, in the context in which Bultmann speaks of a "community in the transcendent," which embraces atheists and nihilists as well as believers, he goes on to ask whether it is really permissible to speak of such a community as a community in God.   His answer to this question is far from a simple affirmative.   He reaffirms his general position that authentic self-surrender is possible only as faith in Jesus Christ and, from this standpoint, proposes that the community of atheists and nihilists and other non-believers is really a community of

[37] *Ibid.*, pp. 176 f.   The passage to which Macquarrie refers here is *Glauben und Verstehen*, II, pp. 271 ff. (pp. 301 ff.).   A little later, he also appeals to Bultmann's *History and Eschatology*, Edinburgh: The University Press, 1957, p. 155.
[38] *Ibid.*, p. 152.   [39] Cf. above, pp. 112, 117, 120-125.

"seeking" for God. This community, then, he clearly distinguishes from a "community of the called," to which believers alone are said to belong.

The same is true of the other passage, where Bultmann speaks of every moment as containing within itself the slumbering possibility of being the eschatological moment, which each individual is summoned to awaken. This statement must be read against the background of its larger context, where it is explicitly stated that this possibility is realised in "Christian faith." To be sure, Bultmann does not say here that this is the *only* way in which the possibility can be realised. But, quite as importantly, he also does not speak of any alternative way for its realisation; and the fairest assumption, surely, is that what he intends to affirm is the same basic position he elsewhere consistently affirms.

Our conclusion is that on this point also Macquarrie's interpretation of Bultmann's proposal is mistaken. He provides no reason whatever for revising the position taken above.

2. THE PROBLEM OF EVALUATING BULTMANN'S PROPOSAL

We have already pointed out that the one important respect in which Macquarrie's second book is different from his first is in its changed position concerning the consistency of Bultmann's proposal. Whereas in the earlier volume, he makes the claim that Bultmann's view is "inconsistent," he now abandons this claim and argues that although Bultmann's view does indeed involve "paradox," this is not the same as logical inconsistency and is, in fact, capable of being "vindicated."[40] He grants, to be sure, that Bultmann's position sometimes gives the impression of inconsistency because of its gratuitous "negations" and "concessions" to secularism, which are

[40] *The Scope of Demythologising*, pp. 222-229, 243; cf. also pp. 26 ff.

entailed by Bultmann's occasional relapses into an uncritical conception of modernity. But, as Macquarrie himself puts it, "once this source of trouble has been tracked down, and once suitable adjustments have been made to meet the various criticisms, there is no difficulty in seeing how the two sides of [Bultmann's] thinking belong naturally together."[41]

The reader will have no difficulty in recognising that this revised evaluation of the consistency of Bultmann's proposal stands in direct conflict with the judgment passed above in Section 8. Perhaps he will be equally quick to recognise that considerations already brought forward in the Appendix suggest the reason Macquarrie's new evaluation must be rejected as inadequate. This reason is twofold : (1) Macquarrie misunderstands the real motive of Bultmann's theology when he attributes to an occasional capitulation to modernity what actually has a far more fundamental basis in Bultmann's understanding of the Christian faith itself ; (2) he imposes on Bultmann's view an explicitness and self-consciousness in which Bultmann himself is completely lacking when he claims that Bultmann deliberately sets a limit to the demand for demythologising and existential interpretation.[42]

We indicated earlier that the reason Bultmann's position must be judged inconsistent is because his appeal to what is, in effect, a mythological understanding of the event of salvation implicitly contradicts his own explicit statements that the demand for demythologising must be "radical" and unlimited. Because Macquarrie misunderstands these statements and, in addition, fails to see that their real basis is in Bultmann's underlying grasp of the Christian kerygma, he reaches the erroneous

---

[41] *Ibid.*, p. 243

[42] It is not clear that this is the *only* reason Macquarrie's judgment must be rejected. In at least one place (cf. *ibid.*, pp. 148 ff.), he seems to take the position of Bultmann that, as applied to the possibility of authentic existence, the distinction between "possibility in principle" and "possibility in fact" need not be (as we have argued) a vacuous distinction. To this extent, his judgment is also open to the objections presented above (cf. pp. 118 ff.).

conclusion that Bultmann's proposal is not really inconsistent at all, even if it involves a necessary but quite legitimate element of "paradox."

In other words, the position Macquarrie "vindicates" against the charge of logical inconsistency is not the position of Bultmann himself, but one that can only be found in his writings because of certain basic misunderstandings. We must conclude, therefore, that Macquarrie's attempt to overthrow the emerging consensus among Bultmann's critics is unsuccessful. The consensus must be reconfirmed and the validity of the argument presented in Section 8 once again asserted.

3. THE PROBLEM OF A TENABLE ALTERNATIVE TO BULTMANN'S PROPOSAL

Because of his revised evaluation of Bultmann's proposal, Macquarrie's own constructive position now seems closer than before to the position of Bultmann himself. Even so, the viewpoint he presents is still essentially the same as in *An Existentialist Theology* ; that is, it is not really the "centre" position of Bultmann, but rather one of the forms of the general position of the "right." The proof of this is that, in a way sharply departing from Bultmann (though Macquarrie, of course, fails to regard it as a departure), he seeks to define the "scope" of demythologising by setting definite limits to thorough-going existential interpretation. Specifically, he argues that such interpretation must be "supplemented" by reference both to (1) a saving act of God, which is "something radically different from and irreducible to a possibility of human existence,"[43] and (2) a unique realisation of authentic self-understanding on the part of the historical person, Jesus of Nazareth.[44]

[43] *Ibid.*, p. 13; cf. pp. 223, 226 f., 128, and 215.
[44] Cf. *ibid.*, pp. 91, n. 1, 95, and 224.

In arguing so, Macquarrie is saying nothing different than he has already said in his earlier volume.[45] And this means that if our criticisms of that volume are correct, they should be equally applicable to this second statement of his position. We propose to show in the remaining paragraphs that this is in fact the case.

It will be recalled that one of our criticisms of the position of the "right" is that it only seems capable of defence by some form of special pleading or fallacious argument. That this criticism also applies to the second formulation of Macquarrie's view is evident from two considerations.

First, there is what appears to be his position concerning the "event" character of Jesus' resurrection. Having stated that "the principal 'events' of which the New Testament speaks —for instance, incarnation, atonement, resurrection—cannot be recognised by historical research as historical events at all," he goes on to claim that "the resurrection is in a slightly different category" from other such events.[46] By this he seems to mean that, while the other events are not historical events at all, the resurrection actually is a historical event, although it cannot be recognised as such by scientific historical research. Thus he speaks of the resurrection as an "unexplained event" or an "inexplicable fact" and suggests that, as such, it "might lead [the scientific historian] to modify his hypothesis that all historical happenings are of the same order." To be sure, Macquarrie grants that the evidence for the "fact" would have to be "very strong" before this decision could be taken. But he also argues that if research "decided that the event was inexplicable, the door would be open for extra-scientific explanations."[47]

Macquarrie's position on this question is admittedly somewhat unclear, and it is possible that our way of restating his view may not be correct. If it is correct, however, the position

---

[45] Cf., e.g., *An Existentialist Theology*, p. 180.
[46] *The Scope of Demythologising*, p. 71.   [47] Cf. *ibid.*, pp. 72 and 71.

he holds now is the same as before, and so is open to identical objections. The notion of an "inexplicable fact" is patently self-contradictory and could not even conceivably warrant the conclusion that there is more than one "order" of historical happenings. What is meant by "fact" is precisely what can somehow be explained within the general limits presupposed by historical research when it looks on history as "a unity in the sense of a closed continuum . . . in which individual events are connected by the succession of cause and effect."[48] What is "inexplicable" within such limits cannot be regarded as fact, but must be treated as fiction or as bare possibility.

In short, when Macquarrie speaks of the resurrection as an "inexplicable fact," he involves himself in the same kind of special pleading as is apparent in his earlier appeal to "historical evidence" that could somehow have force without being confirmed on "general grounds of probability."[49]

The judgment implied here receives additional support from yet a second consideration. This is the way Macquarrie undertakes to argue that "existential interpretation needs to be supplemented by some factual historical assertions," that is, by "a 'minimum core of factuality,' the overwhelming probability of which may, prior to any research, be claimed on the basis of a rational inference from the presence before our eyes of the Christian community with its documents and traditions."[50] So stated, Macquarrie's argument is modest enough, and it is difficult to take issue with its basic point. But this can hardly be said of the very different statement of the argument with which (without any indication on his part that this is the case!) he repeatedly confuses the initial statement. He also attempts to argue that theology to-day can "assure itself that the way of life which it commends is a possibility in 'real' life" only if it is possible to point to "an actual instance within history of the kind of life which the

---

[48] So Bultmann in *Existence and Faith*, p. 291.   [49] Cf. above, p. 135.
[50] *The Scope of Demythologising*, p. 245; cf. also pp. 73 ff.

kerygma proclaims."[51]   Unless we can assert that "there really
was this kind of person, that this possible way of life has
actually been exhibited in history," authentic existence is
"only a remote ideal . . . on which no one could embark with
any confidence."[52]

Aside from the question of whether any historian could
possibly tell us that a historical figure did or did not have a
certain *existentiell* self-understanding, Macquarrie's second
argument is open to the most serious objections. Indeed, when
he asks rhetorically, "How can we know what can be done
except on the basis of what has been done?"[53] his case ceases
even to be plausible. For surely all of us can think of countless exceptions to the rule he implies. Consider, for example,
a research team working to break through to a cure for cancer.
Does their obvious "confidence" that such a cure can be
found have the basis that Macquarrie would have us believe?
Furthermore, does the fact itself of a possibility once being
actualised in any way give "assurance" that it can be realised
again by us? Is not one of the most indubitable truths of our
experience that all sorts of things have been done—say, com-
posing poems of the stature of Homer's—that we ourselves
can have no hope of doing at all?

In face of such transparent difficulties as these, one finds it
hard to avoid the conclusion that Macquarrie is engaged in a
desperate attempt to salvage what otherwise threatens to be
lost to a critical historical approach to theological problems.
In any case, the second form of his argument for a "minimum
core of factuality" is fallacious, and, since it is the only argument he offers, his position at this point seems indefensible.[54]

There is a second criticism that we previously made of the
position of the "right," and so also of Macquarrie's own

---

[51] *Ibid.*, pp. 99 and 91, n. 1.   [52] *Ibid.*, pp. 95 and 98.   [53] *Ibid*, p. 90.
[54] It is interesting that Macquarrie refers in this connection (cf. *ibid.*, pp. 91,
n. 1 and 245) to James M. Robinson's *New Quest of the Historical Jesus*, London:
S.C.M. Press, Ltd., 1959, since the position of Robinson himself is vulnerable
to parallel objections.

earlier statements. This is the weightier criticism that such a position is finally unable to give adequate expression to the Christian faith itself. In this respect also, there are two indications that Macquarrie's second book is open to objection.

In the first place, there is his repeated statement that existential interpretation has to be "supplemented" by reference to "a saving act of God" that is "radically different" from a possibility of human existence. That Macquarrie should even speak in this way is itself sufficient to cause misgivings about the adequacy of his position. For, in the understanding of faith, reference to God and to his saving action is hardly a "supplement" to a proper analysis of man and his possibilities of self-understanding. The issue between a humanistic philosophy of existence and authentic Christian faith is considerably more subtle than Macquarrie appears to suppose. What faith regards as inadequate in such a philosophy is not simply that it fails to make reference to God, while speaking correctly about man, but that it does not even speak about man himself in an adequate way—or, alternatively, that if it does speak about man correctly, it is also making a reference to God that it fails to make properly explicit. In other words, as faith understands them, God and man are of such nature and are so related that to speak adequately of either is in fact to speak of both. For this reason, we must reassert against Macquarrie that " 'statements about God and his activity' *are* 'statements about human existence,' and *vice versa*."[55]

The great virtue of existential philosophy as a theological resource is that it provides a conceptuality in which this point can be expressed in a way appropriate to faith's own understanding. To be sure, we have argued that Bultmann makes less than maximum use of this resource because he fails consistently to acknowledge the full scope of the philosophical task. Because of his legitimate concern that God be not robbed of his "subjectivity," he is sometimes misled to deny

[55] Cf. above, p. 137.

that God as well as man is necessarily involved in any valid existential analysis. Even so, we have also taken pains to make clear that the remedy for this weakness is quite different than many of the critics on the "right" would have us believe. What is required is not that existential interpretation be "supplemented," but that its own implicit reference to God and his saving action be fully and consistently explicated.[56]

Macquarrie himself occasionally seems to want to make this very point—as, for instance, when he argues that such concepts as "God," "act of God," and "existence" involve a polarity of opposites within a whole.[57] Nevertheless, most of his statements appear to point to the quite different position we have been criticising. This is especially true of his discussion with Buri and Jaspers, where he seems all but unable to recognise that the view these men attempt to develop is radically different not only from a mythological "objectivism," but also from the "subjectivism" of a position such as Jean Paul Sartre's and other forms of truncated humanism. He grants that both men speak of "grace" and of the "gift-like character of authentic existence"; but he also insists that they fail to make clear their intention to speak of a saving act of God of the kind of which faith itself knows and speaks.[58] One cannot help but wonder what Buri and Jaspers would have to say to reassure Macquarrie about their intention. In any case, his own grasp on an alternative to an inadequate "objectivism" is most uncertain, and much that he says would have to be qualified if it is in the direction of such an alternative that he wishes to move.

A second indication of the inadequacy of Macquarrie's position is his consistent affirmation that existential interpretation also needs to be "supplemented" by reference to a "minimum core of factuality," by which he means the person of the historical Jesus and, more particularly, Jesus' having

[56] Cf. above, pp. 152 f.   [57] Cf. *The Scope of Demythologising*, pp. 240 ff.
[58] Cf. *ibid.*, p. 151; also pp. 129-185 *passim*.

actualised an authentic self-understanding. Macquarrie rejects the view, to be sure, that Jesus is the only channel whereby grace and revelation are communicated to men, and he explicitly assures us that, if this is Bultmann's view, he has no alternative but to disagree with it.[59] But one hardly knows what to make of this assurance in view of his obvious concern to argue that faith as authentic self-understanding has to be "supplemented" by an appeal to the historical Jesus. We have already seen that his argument to this effect is fallacious and that on this ground alone his position is incapable of defence. But the far weightier objection to the argument is that it seems to violate faith's own understanding of man before God. Is not the demand for such a "supplement" an implicit denial of man's radical freedom and responsibility and God's even more radical freedom and transcendence ? Is it not, in short, a breach of the Reformation principles of *sola gratia—sola fide* ?

So it seems, at least, to us. And it is for this reason, finally, more than for any other, that we are forced to take issue with Macquarrie's position.

[59] Cf. *ibid.*, pp. 176 f.

Bibliography

Index

BIBLIOGRAPHY

The following books referred to in the footnotes have appeared in British editions :

JOHN BAILLIE, *Our Knowledge of God*, Oxford University Press, 1939.

JOHN BAILLIE, *The Place of Jesus in Modern Christianity*, T. & T. Clark, 1929.

H. W. BARTSCH (ed.), *Kerygma and Myth*, S.P.C.K., 1953.

GÜNTHER BORNKAMM, *Jesus of Nazareth*, Hodder & Stoughton, 1960.

EMIL BRUNNER, *The Divine-Human Encounter*, S.C.M. Press, Ltd., 1944.

EMIL BRUNNER, *The Christian Doctrine af Creation and Redemption*, Lutterworth Press, 1952.

RUDOLF BULTMANN, *Theology of the New Testament*, S.C.M. Press, Ltd., 1952, 1955.

RUDOLF BULTMANN, *Jesus Christ and Mythology*, S.C.M. Press, Ltd., 1960.

RUDOLF BULTMANN, *The Presence of Eternity: History & Eschatology*, Edinburgh University Press.

RUDOLF BULTMANN, *Existence and Faith*, Hodder & Stoughton, 1961.

RUDOLF BULTMANN, *Primitive Christianity in its Contemporary Setting*, Fontana Books, 1960.

GERAINT VAUGHAN JONES, *Christology and Myth in the New Testament*, Allen and Unwin, 1956.

CHARLES HARTSHORNE, *The Divine Relativity*, Oxford University Press, 1948.

C. W. KEGLEY and R. W. BRETALL (eds.), *The Theology of Paul Tillich*, Macmillan Co., New York, 1952.

JOHN KNOX, *The Death of Christ*, Collins, 1959.

WALTER LEIBRECHT (ed.), *Religion and Culture : Essays in Honour of Paul Tillich*, S.C.M. Press, Ltd., 1959.

JOHN MACQUARRIE, *The Scope of Demythologising : Bultmann and His Critics*, S.C.M. Press, Ltd., 1960.

Bibliography

F. D. MAURICE, *Theological Essays*, Clarke & Co., Ltd., 1956.

GIOVANNI MIEGGE, *Gospel and Myth in the Theology of Rudolf Bultmann*, Lutterworth Press, 1960.

REINHOLD NIEBUHR, *The Nature and Destiny of Man*, Nisbet & Co., Ltd., 1955.

ARTHUR SMETHURST, *Modern Science and Christian Beliefs*, Nisbet & Co., Ltd., 1955.

R. GREGOR SMITH, *The New Man: Christianity and Man's Coming of Age*, S.C.M. Press, Ltd., 1956.

PAUL TILLICH, *Systematic Theology*, Nisbet & Co., Ltd., 1953.

INDEX